THE
PLEASURE
SELLER

The Pleasure Seller

John C. Souter

Tyndale House
Publishers, Inc.
Wheaton, Illinois

Note: The names of many of Bruce's friends
have been changed—to protect the guilty!

The Pleasure Seller was first published
by Inspiration House Publishers, Inc., Wildomar, California.
This Tyndale House Publishers, Inc., edition
is produced by arrangement with
Inspiration House Publishers, Inc.

Library of Congress Catalog Card Number 78-58749
ISBN: 0-8423-4839-5, paper.
Copyright© 1977, John C. Souter.
All rights reserved.
First Tyndale House printing,
January, 1979.
Printed in the United States of America.

CONTENTS

Garden Grove
THE *ORANGE COUNTY* EVENING *NEWS*

134 PAGES   GARDEN GROVE, CALIFORNIA, WEDNESDAY, DECEMBER 17, 1969

Police Raid Opium Pad
1 Block from Station

Three Arrests Made So Far

By RAY MERCHANT

Opium and marijuana were confiscated by police Tuesday night in a raid on a "pad" only a block away from the Garden Grove police station.

Detectives found 2½ ounces of opium, offered to them at $10 a gram or $90 an ounce, with a street value of some $800, and a "quantity" of marijuana.

Three arrests were made.

Undercover Garden Grove and Buena Park detectives termed the opium find rare in that it was the first time they had found any here.

Booked at Orange County Jail on charges of suspicion of sale of opium and possession of marijuana were Kenneth P. Sommers, 23, 11401 Garden Grove Blvd., address of the "pad"; Bruce J. Dzandzara, 21, 11251 Motz St., Garden Grove, and David L. Kay, 21, no address.

Garden Grove detectives said warrants are pending against "several" more Garden Grove residents.

The "bust" culminated a six-week investigation conducted in the Garden Grove Euclid Park area by Buena Park detectives, who had been making buys.

PISTOL DISCHARGED

They went to the Garden Grove Boulevard house with Sommers and Kay on the guise of buying opium at $90 an ounce.

According to the police report, when the two men checked, they found they didn't have enough money to make the buy. One detective reached in his coat pocket to pull out his .25-caliber pistol. It caught on the

See: "Opium," Page A-2

OPIUM

Continued from Page A-1

edge of his pocket, fell to the floor and discharged.

Garden Grove detectives waiting outside heard the shot and rushed inside. No one was hurt. The arrests were made immediately, and the three suspects were transported to Orange County Jail.

Buena Park detectives, working undercover on another probe, were led to the Garden Grove case by an informant.

After they had made contact with the Garden Grove suspects, the detectives then contacted Garden Grove police and asked for backup support in making the raid.

Chapter One
The Opium Bust

The designs on the oriental tapestry hanging from the ceiling were beginning to move. I amused myself by making the patterns change form and color. Every line, every thread, every detail on that intricately woven fabric was coming into focus with microscopic accuracy.

The ordinary things in the room around me had now turned into objects of exquisite beauty. The dull-gray world had been made over by the surrealistic images in front of my eyes. I enjoyed being high on LSD.

Pleasurable thoughts flooded my mind. Bill and I

had just moved into our own place. Now we would have real freedom. There would be lots of wild parties in this place. Bill was already in the next room with a pick-up.

We were drug dealers, and business had never been better; lately we had earned thousands selling dope. I began to daydream about my future wealth.

A beautiful rainbow formed in my head. At the ray's end was a glistening pot of gold with coins falling all around me. They were so real I could touch them.

A knock at the front door interrupted my dreams. Through the screen I saw a familiar face.

"Is Nam here?"

"No, Terry, he's out somewhere," I lied. I knew Bill wouldn't want any interruptions.

"Do you know where he is? He was going to sell to these guys out here."

Dollar signs flashed into my brain. I might as well cash in on this situation. A red Chevy Super Sport sat across the street. There were four guys in it.

"I don't know where Nam is, but I can get any drug they want."

We walked out to the car, and my acid-soaked brain vibrated. Several cars drove by, and the headlights formed a series of still images in front of my eyes. People walking down the street looked plastic. I carefully surveyed the street for police.

"What's happening?" I quizzed the driver with a smile from ear to ear. I was too loaded to know what was really happening.

"Where's Nam?" he asked.

"He's out somewhere. I hear you want to buy some stuff."

"Yeah," the driver answered. "I'm the big daddy at the park with all the bucks." His words sounded a little melodramatic but I was too high to care. "We want to get loaded. What have you got?"

My LSD-controlled brain enlarged each face in the car to the size of a poster. I studied every expression. None of them had long hair.

"Do you want hash?"

"No. What else you got?"

"Grass? Reds? Speed? Acid?" I gave them a long list of drugs, but they weren't interested in anything I offered. "How about opium?"

"Opium? Hey, that sounds good. That's what we want. How much?"

"Ninety dollars an ounce." At that price I would make a heavy profit.

"That's good. Do you have it in the house?"

"No, it's at a friend's place, but I can take you there."

"Okay, get in," the driver said.

"Don't get in, they're cops!" Terry blurted before the driver could open the door.

Everybody in the car started laughing. I looked at him, then back at them. "These guys can't be cops," I reasoned.

I climbed into the back seat between two of them. We drove off leaving Terry standing on the curb. Everyone was guzzling beer and swearing as they talked. The driver was all over the road. He was blowing my mind.

"Hey, maintain. You don't want to be pulled over with these beers in the car."

"No problem," the driver responded.

My companions began to look older and older. On

first impression they looked like my friends, but the wrinkles around their eyes were growing.

A strange feeling suddenly engulfed me. I was getting strong vibrations that something bad was going to happen, and there was nothing I could do about it.

We arrived at my friend's house and climbed out of the car. "Only two of you can come in," I announced. "My friend doesn't want a lot of company."

I wasn't certain if my contact still had the opium because it had been several weeks since we had last done business. I knocked on Jeff's door and he invited us in.

Jeff's place resembled an oriental harem. The walls and ceiling were covered with Turkish tapestries and black light posters. Up on a shelf I spotted the opium wrapped in aluminum foil.

While Jeff and I talked, the buyers were surveying the room. One picked up a hash pipe and commented on how far out it was. Without any warning, the other man threw his beer across the room, reached into his shirt, and pulled out a gun.

"Narcotics agents—hold it!" he yelled.

As he pulled out his gun and cocked it, the pistol snagged on his shirt and flipped from his hand. It hit the floor and discharged.

"*Bang!*"

The sound blasted my ears, and the acid in my system caused the noise to reverberate through my head. I couldn't tell whether the bullet had hit me.

"Oh my God!" yelled one of the men outside.

My mind freaked out. I was totally confused. The other agent pointed his gun at me, and with the hammer cocked, yelled, "Hold it, you hippie, or I'll kill you right now!'' I was shaking so badly I couldn't have resisted.

The first narc reached for the drugs. ''Opium,'' he smiled as he smelled it.

The agents who had been outside rushed into the house, and in seconds the Garden Grove police arrived.

''What a bummer,'' I said to Jeff under my breath.

''Don't worry,'' he whispered back, ''it's not opium.''

''You sure? Man, it looks like the opium.'' I was almost certain it was the drug we had been selling and getting high on for months.

We were taken to the Garden Grove police station. As we were being processed into the jail, a cop pointed at me. ''You're on a drug, aren't you? You're high.''

Anyone could have seen I was on something. I was starting to come down but my eyes were still dilated.

''I'm not on anything,'' I lied. ''I'm scared, that's all.''

''You're loaded,'' he challenged.

''I'm not loaded, really.''

''Ah, it's probably some psychedelic, and we couldn't find it in your bloodstream anyway.'' He let it drop.

Jeff and I assured each other we would keep our mouths shut. They led us into separate rooms for questioning. When they began to interrogate me, I clammed up.

''Where'd you get the opium?''

''I don't know anything. I want to see a lawyer.'' I was determined not to tell on my friend.

''Look, Danzara, if you're cooperative, we can

get you out of this thing with no record at all. Where's Bill? He's the man we really want."

"I don't know where he is."

"Come on, Bruce, you just got in the way. Bill is the guy we really want. Tell us where he is, and we'll get you off."

"I told you, I don't know where he is."

"Look at this," he said, pulling out some heroin. "I busted this from some guys tonight, some of your friends from the park. I'm busting everybody; you might as well start talking and save yourself, 'cause everybody's going to end up in jail.

"You're going to prison for five years. There's no doubt in my mind you're going to the joint. Selling opium is a state offense. When the judge hears the word 'opium' you've had it. It's not like marijuana."

I knew he was right, but I remembered my friend had said it really wasn't opium. This cop wasn't going to talk me into anything.

"Look," I said, "if I want to talk, how can I get hold of you?" I had no intention of telling anything to this cop, but I didn't want him to issue a bad report on me. He gave me his card.

We were transferred quickly to Orange County Jail in Santa Ana. They made us shower and change our clothes. Our belongings were taken away and we were given levis, sweat shirts, and sandals to wear. We were photographed and fingerprinted. It was the first time I had been booked.

I was placed in a large cell with Jeff. Fear nagged my brain. The gnawing threat of a long prison term was like a dark cloud over my head.

"Jeff, what was that stuff?"

"It wasn't opium," he insisted.

"What was it then?"

"It's incense. It's Sundance Incense from India. It's oily and looks like opium."

I just couldn't believe it was incense. I wondered whether Jeff was lying.

The next morning my father came to visit me. From the pained look on his face, it was obvious he was depressed. He had a look which proclaimed, "I've failed as a father."

My dad held up the front page of the *Orange County News*. The headline read, "POLICE RAID OPIUM PAD ONE BLOCK FROM STATION, Two Arrests Made So Far."

I was shocked; we made the front page headlines. The article didn't have all the facts correct, but it was where the whole county could see it. "Everybody's gonna know I'm in jail," I said to myself. "What are my girl friend's parents gonna say?"

I spent most of the next week in jail. Each hour seemed like a day. Christmas was coming and I wanted desperately to be free. The idle hours without drugs made me reflect on the past.

Chapter Two
A Little Help
From My Friends

I was born in Southern California, and I lived most of my life in Garden Grove. My childhood was not unusual and I had no traumatic experiences.

My parents and most of my relatives were religious people. I attended a parochial school through the eighth grade. This school had high academic standards and taught us to believe in God.

In ninth grade I began to attend a public high school in Garden Grove, but still went to church faithfully. I studied the doctrines of the church I attended, but this study eventually caused me to formulate serious questions about the church. The God to whom I was exposed seemed to contradict himself. I began to doubt the doctrines of the church, and almost overnight stopped attending altogether.

In my senior year in high school, a friend called me on the phone.

"Hi, Bruce, this is Brad."

"Oh hi, Brad. What's up?"

"Hey man, I'm over at Wilson's house. We're having a party, and we just smoked marijuana."

"Really?"

"Yeah. Man, it's great. I feel like I'm floating. Why don't I come over and you can try it?"

"No, I don't want to get into that."

"It won't hurt you. I'll come over and show ya."

I wasn't certain what marijuana was or what it did to you, but I feared it as something evil and dangerous because of the publicity it had received. I was surprised at the appearance of the marijuana Brad produced that night.

"Here, take it. It won't hurt you."

"You sure?"

"Yeah. It hasn't hurt me."

Brad certainly looked normal. If he had received

any bad effects, they didn't show. He described the good sensations he was experiencing, and his words were quite convincing. I decided it couldn't be as bad as everyone claimed.

"Okay, give it to me."

I smoked pot that night, but nothing happened. In the next few days I tried two more times, but still nothing happened. I figured marijuana must be pretty harmless, and if I ever did get high, there probably wouldn't be much to it.

A few days later Brad and I went into a friend's garage to smoke grass again. This time something happened—I got high. I felt as if I were in a boat. Everything rocked gently back and forth as if I were suspended a little above earth.

When we ate dinner, I couldn't believe the taste of the food—it was ten times better than normal. My senses seemed alive for the first time. Never had I experienced anything like this. Brad had been right.

Marijuana was so pleasurable I began to use it often. Many of my high school friends also used it, and we began to smoke it together. We would light one joint at a time and pass it around until everyone was high.

Sometimes we entered restaurants in a state of euphoria and would start laughing. Once we started, we couldn't stop. After several minutes, fear that the manager would call the police would cause us to leave even before we ordered.

Now that I was involved with an illegal drug, I began to listen carefully to the public reaction against drug abuse. I took note of the stories on the radio about LSD. People supposedly jumped out of high buildings or turned into human vegetables. But the stories didn't scare me because I had heard similar claims about marijuana, and they had not been true.

Pot had done many good things for me. It increased my appetite and awareness of the world. It helped me think about issues that had never been of interest to me before. It helped me break out of my sheltered existence.

A friend named Jim who had run away from home to the Haight-Ashbury district of San Francisco returned with many heavy stories about LSD. I sat with ten high school buddies one night listening to this hippie tell his tales. Eight of us decided to try acid that night.

Jim had been using LSD for over a year and had built up a resistance. He gave us larger dosages than we needed. Still, each of us received an amount smaller than a match head. A little extra was left, so I took it to make certain I got high. We piled into two cars and drove off to a drive-in for our first psychedelic trip.

As we pulled into the theater, my first illusions began to appear. The parking area was covered with popcorn, paper cups, and boxes. When I examined the asphalt a second time, it had turned to black velvet. The trash was transformed into brilliant gems of every description. I saw emeralds, rubies, and diamonds, depending on the color of the trash. I was overwhelmed by the beauty.

We pulled into our parking spaces, and somebody suggested we hit the head while we still could. Entering the men's rest room, every molecule of my body began to quiver and vibrate. I was experiencing an electric feeling.

18

I turned on the faucet and saw the water had turned plastic. Fascinated by its elasticity, I pulled at it with my fingers until it dawned on me that every man in the head was staring in my direction.

Looking around, I discovered my friends had gone. Leaving the rest room, the beautiful patterns in the snack bar rug overwhelmed me in a forest of brilliant color. I began to leap over the different hues in my path. Everything was happening too fast. The visuals before my eyes were so amplified I was having difficulty handling them. I glanced up to discover hundreds of people in the snack bar, all staring at me. Outside, the cars were arranged in a large bubble, as though I were looking through a fish-eye lens. Every light was flashing directly into my eyes. The world was exploding.

I couldn't remember where we were parked, so for 45 minutes, I wandered around the drive-in searching for my friends. Those two cars represented safety and I had to find them.

"Wow, there he is," someone said as I approached.

"Man, I got lost." I would never leave that car again.

Everyone was smoking and when we moved our cigarettes through the air funny little trails were created. These light streaks disappeared slowly, and we began to write in the air. We became all tangled in them.

I closed my eyes and a bizarre world appeared. Anything I thought about instantly became a visual picture. Paisleys, patterns, rainbows, and numbers floated in and out of my mind. If I thought about someone, his face appeared with intricate detail. Any period of history I remembered flashed in like a fully-costumed motion picture.

When I looked up at the movie screen, I became part of the film. It was a comedy about a janitor who reluctantly became an astronaut. I became that man, because I, too, was experiencing something new and exciting. But a problem developed in the astronaut's spacecraft, and he was told, "You're never going to come back." Those words were repeated over and over in my brain as if I were never going to return to normal.

Somehow one of my friends drove home that night. When I slipped into bed I was still hallucinating. I desperately wanted it all to end, but I couldn't shut off the images.

The next morning my mind had returned to normal but my body felt strange. For two long months my arms and legs felt numb. I became convinced these leftover symptoms were psychological. None of my friends had developed this problem, and I concluded one more trip would take away the numbness. I dropped LSD a second time, and the feeling returned.

My second experience with acid was quite pleasurable, so I began to take the high-powered drug regularly. Over the next year I took thirty trips. I was also smoking between 10 and 15 joints a day.

At first it was difficult to obtain enough drugs to keep myself high. But I searched quietly for people who could supply quantities of grass and acid and eventually came up with what I needed.

This new life-style brought few changes to my life at first, but over the months, my value system changed. Everyday life no longer worried me. My problems weren't so big, and I became much more concerned about national affairs and the war in Viet

Nam. LSD made me aware of the injustices in the world and caused me to develop a new attitude towards our society.

"Why can't we just love everybody?" I preached to my friends. "I want to turn everyone on to the good life."

On the Fourth of July after graduation, Brad invited me to a party given by some of his friends. When we entered the house, I was surprised to see adults. The owner of the home had provided several alcoholic beverages for the young people. The party was extremely crowded, and most of our friends were in the backyard smoking pot. After getting high, I started searching for a chick.

Wandering around, I noticed an attractive girl in the living room. She had dark brown hair to her waist and was wearing a tight sweater and pants. She stood about five feet three inches tall, but the thing that set her apart was her catlike eyes. She noticed me looking at her and smiled. Somehow I made my way through the crowd to her.

"Hi; my name's Bruce."

"Hi, Bruce," she replied sweetly. "My name is Sharon. Are you high on some kind of drug? Your eyes look funny."

"I've been drinking all night, and I just smoked some weed."

"Do you smoke it often?" she quizzed innocently.

"I've been getting loaded for about a year."

It was difficult for Sharon to imagine anyone taking drugs for over a year. I seemed to her a man of the world. Still, I could tell she was attracted to me, and we spent the rest of the evening together.

Late that night when I arrived home, I was too

high and tired to remove my father's car keys from my pocket. At 3 A.M. he rose for work. When he didn't find his car keys, he searched my pants. He located his keys, but also discovered four joints.

The next morning, I could barely remember the night before. The image of a pretty girl with sexy eyes was still in my brain, but I couldn't be certain it hadn't been a dream. I couldn't remember her name.

Suddenly I remembered my dad's keys. Reaching for my pants revealed the keys and my joints had vanished. My dad had discovered them. "Does he have any idea what they are?" I wondered. "I've got to remove the evidence."

Quickly I ransacked our house. I discovered his hiding place and then dashed off to the store to purchase catnip. Returning, I replaced each joint with a fake.

That afternoon dad returned from work and came into my room. "What were doing with that stuff last night?" he questioned.

"What stuff?" I responded innocently.

"You know what I mean."

"Oh, you mean the catnip? We were just messing around. We were playing games."

"Yeah, I know, I lit one."

My heart did a quick flip-flop at his statement.

"At first I was afraid it was marijuana," he went on, "but it wasn't. I smelled it, and it wasn't. Bruce, I don't want you messing around with drugs."

"Oh, I won't, Dad," I lied, breathing a sigh of relief.

My dad had smelled the real stuff and hadn't realized what it was. I was safe for the moment, but I knew he would continue to watch me.

During the next week I questioned my friends

about the girl at the party, but no one knew her name. Two weeks later, at the hamburger stand near my house, I peered through the order-window, and there she was. She looked great in her simple white uniform.

Our eyes met and she gave me a warm smile. Darting out front, she enveloped me in her arms. Her affectionate greeting surprised me.

"Oh Bruce, I missed you so. Why didn't you call me?"

"I couldn't remember your name. None of my friends knew your name."

"I'll fix that," she said. "My name is Sharon. Do you have a piece of paper? I'll give you my phone number."

There was a strong physical attraction between Sharon and me. We didn't have to put it into words. We both felt it. When we had been going together for three months, we began to make love. We cared deeply for each other, and it seemed so natural.

I was preparing for college, and Sharon was starting her senior year in high school. She was a cheerleader and had never been involved with drugs of any kind. I tried to convince Sharon she should take drugs. I wanted her mind and feelings where mine were.

One night I insisted she try some weed.

"Go on, take it."

"Well, okay, if you're sure it won't hurt me."

"Of course it won't hurt you. You know I wouldn't do anything to hurt you. Go on, take a drag."

Sharon liked it. It wasn't long before she smoked grass every time we went out.

Chapter Three
The Pleasure Seller

A steady girl friend created a need for money. I soon discovered when I purchased large quantities of drugs I could sell the surplus. Selling drugs had many advantages. I had no boss, no hours, and no taxes to pay. My popularity increased because I could give free dope to my friends, but the most exciting part of my new occupation was the income.

During my freshman year of college I met a student named Brian Young. Brian was of medium height with blond hair and blue eyes. We quickly became friends and started getting loaded together.

Brian invited me to his house, where he lived with his parents, sister, four brothers, and eight foster boys. The foster kids were the kind of incorrigibles no one else would take.

I was astonished at the permissive atmosphere in Brian's house. Mr. Young openly sanctioned drug-taking and dealing. If any of the boys living in the house desired to take a girl to bed, there were no restrictions. The only thing prohibited was physical violence.

Mr. Young's hair had grown to his shoulders and he parted his foot-long beard in the Babylonian style. He was six feet, six inches tall and weighed at least 250 pounds. His rugged frame made him invincible. Sometimes gangs would try to crash a Young party, and he would assault them with unusual fury. He possessed superhuman power and endurance and always maintained firm physical control over his house.

Mr. Young was regarded with sinister reverence by all those who came to his house. He never sold drugs, and no one ever saw him use them, but he thoroughly approved of dope. He often preached about drugs and God in his living room. He knew the Bible and easily proved his points from it.

I really dug Mr. Young's profound monologues, but he was doing more than propagating his philosophy; he was playing with our minds. He would work us into a heavy discussion, then abruptly change the subject or walk out of the room in mid-sentence. When high, our minds could not adjust to such radical changes.

The freedom the Young household offered was very appealing, but as I began to spend more time there, Sharon expressed a strong disapproval of Brian and his family. She wanted nothing to do with them, and so I could do whatever I desired at Brian's place without fear Sharon would find out. Each night after my date with her was over, Brian and I would go out and pick up chicks. Almost all the girls we met used dope, and if they went with us they got free drugs in return for what we wanted.

I began to take some capsules known as red devils. Reds are the street name for seconal, a barbiturate. The drug affected my body like alcohol and often caused me to become belligerent.

After using reds heavily for a month, I developed a physical dependency on the drug. Addiction scared me, as I always maintained I was free to quit any time. I completely stopped taking reds. My body began to ache from withdrawal, so I took other drugs to ease the pain. Once over the dependence, I was careful to avoid becoming strung out again.

Brian, however, had become a red freak. He was injecting the drug directly into his blood stream and was getting so loaded he could barely function. He even went out of his way to steal from his friends when he was stoned.

The Young family had become quite well known to the Garden Grove police. Patrol cars constantly cruised their street because of the endless stream of parties. Eventually, two permanent roadblocks were set up on both ends of the street in front of their house. Anyone coming or going was halted and checked for drugs, and the girls were constantly picked up on curfew violations. But police activity did not curb the constant party atmosphere.

One night we decided to try something different. We had forty kilos (bricks) of marijuana, so we decided to put a butane torch to one of them—several hundred dollars' worth of weed. The smoke quickly filled the room and everyone simply inhaled to get high.

We smoked pot with everything. No matter whether we were high on acid, reds, or wine, grass always mellowed the trip and made it more pleasurable.

Several of us also became hash freaks. Hashish is a derivative of the marijuana plant, ten times more powerful than good marijuana. An ounce of hash in a hash pipe would be passed between five or six of us. Hard on the lungs and throat, we smoked hash until someone passed out. It became a game to see who would pass out first.

Sometimes we'd obtain hash oil, another derivative of marijuana, which is ten to twenty times as powerful as hashish. We would blend hashish into a joint, then rub hash oil on the cigarette paper. This combination was so potent we didn't just get high, we hallucinated as if we were on acid.

While taking all these drugs, I was trying to finish my second year of junior college. I was taking sixteen units and had to rise early each morning to attend class. Sharon, who had graduated from high school and was now attending college with me, appeared each morning at my parents' house to drag me out of bed and make certain I made it to class on time. Even with her help, my foggy mind barely made it through the year.

Sharon and I were making love regularly without taking any precautions against pregnancy. When she missed her second period we both became concerned. I put off doing anything, hoping the problem would go away. I almost told my father, then decided against it.

After she had missed three periods and was definitely getting sick every morning, I took her to a doctor. The tests were positive. Sharon was pregnant.

I prayed that night. It was my first prayer in some time. "God, I don't want to marry Sharon. Please help me, God. I'll make a deal with you. If Sharon has a miscarriage or something, I'll stop messing around and settle down."

Next morning she called. "Guess what? I started my period this morning!"

"You're kidding! Did you have a miscarriage?"

"No, I just started my period, just like normal. The doctor must have been wrong."

I was overjoyed, elated. I couldn't believe my luck.

By now I was selling so heavily it was difficult to keep my drugs hidden. I was afraid to put them all in one place in our house for fear my parents or brother would discover them and wipe me out of business. I began to hide my supplies in every good location I could conjure up. I taped them under the coffee table and other living room furniture. I put several kilos in the crawl space under the house. I even hid some pills in the lining of my mother's old clothes.

In the backyard I was growing marijuana everywhere. I concealed my plants by putting them behind other plants in the garden. I hid several cans which contained small sprouts on the roof.

I was able to maintain an appearance of sobriety in front of my parents even when loaded. They didn't have any idea I was a doper. But the more I sold, the more foot traffic came through our house. All kinds of friends came to see me but stayed only a few minutes. My parents soon became suspicious. One day I came home to find my father had discovered my marijuana plants in the backyard. He had uprooted and destroyed all of them. He had also searched through the house and had found many of my other drugs.

Once my parents realized I was using and selling drugs, they began to hassle me. My dad and I began to have frequent arguments. One day we clashed in front of my friends. He challenged my whole philosophy of life, including my attitude toward communal living which he said I picked up from my Marxist professors at school.

"You're a communist and a drug-taker!" he yelled.

"Well, you're an American imperialist!" I shouted back. "You're a fascist John Bircher!"

With one bone-jarring blow, my dad smacked me on the jaw and knocked me across the room and through the screen door. Luckily the glass door was open. Dad pursued me outside and challenged me to swing back, but I knew better than try. He had boxed in the army.

"That's what I mean! All your generation understands is force! You just don't know how to love."

I stalked off with my friends.

One night right before I drove up to Brian's place, five police cars screeched to a halt in front of his house. I kept driving. Looking in my rearview mirror, I saw police and narcotics officers swarm around the house. They smashed the door open, kicked in the windows, and arrested everyone in the building.

Brian later told me he had received a phone call before the police arrived. Someone had checked on the availability of drugs. Sensing something was wrong, he told everyone to flush their dope down the toilet. No one stayed in jail long because of Brian's quick thinking. There was not enough evidence in the house.

The Youngs moved within the city to a larger place, with a swimming pool, a large spacious backyard, and a small house in back where the foster kids lived. We continued to party almost every night, and now went "skinny-dipping" in the pool. There was always a good time at the Young's.

Brian and I went to one of our connections to help him break down synthetic mescaline (a psychedelic like LSD) into capsules containing one trip each. While we worked with the drug, it began to be absorbed through our skin. We each swallowed a

29

capsule to get high, and discovered we had mistakenly taken the undiluted amounts containing fifty doses each! Things soon began to spin.

Brian passed out, and his head fell into a bowl of mescaline. The drug was up in his nose and mouth. I pulled his head out of the bowl, and he regained consciousness.

We were both too loaded to go home; so we spaced out on the floor. For two days I was unable to see. When I opened my eyes, I saw only brilliant white light. On this screen, I could mentally create one cartoon image after another until my trip ended three days later and we both went home.

Sharon and I often double-dated with another couple. One night these friends, Phil and Diane, had a quarrel. I saw Phil later at a party and could tell he wanted to take on the world. He was a red freak and was holding a beer in his hand.

"I'm gonna drop Diane and start living it up," he announced with slurred speech. "What do I need her for anyway?"

"Diane loves you, Phil. You don't want to drop her."

He thought for a few moments, then started to cry. "You're right. I do love Diane. I think I'll go back over there tonight."

He stopped talking and fell over quietly on his side.

"Phil? Phil? You awake!"

He was snoring gently, and I decided not to wake him. The party was still going on loudly around us, but it was time for me to go home.

The next day, when I returned from school,

Sharon met me at my house. Her face was white.

"Phil Jones is dead."

"You're kidding! I just saw him last night."

"He died in his sleep."

"Oh, my God."

The combination of reds and alcohol depressed Phil's system and his heart stopped while he slept. I was the last person to see him alive.

Most of my friends came to Phil's funeral. When Sharon and I walked into the mortuary, Diane met us. She was weeping when she hugged me.

I became unnerved by the coffin's presence in the next room. I stumbled into the chapel and peered into the casket. Phil looked as if he were sleeping. I expected his chest to fill with breath and his eyes to open, but his lifeless form lay there quietly. The finality of death overwhelmed me.

Phil's sudden demise caught me by surprise. I was filled with fear of dying by a drug overdose. But it was not death I feared; it was what would happen afterwards. I didn't know whether I was destined for heaven or hell—or whether I would simply cease to exist altogether.

At Brian's place several months later, I met a Viet Nam veteran named Bill. He was five feet seven inches tall and of slender build, but he was dangerously hot-headed and would challenge the world when he was stoned.

Nam, as Bill was nicknamed, possessed several special joints called Nookmaus. They were professionally rolled joints, soaked in opium, which he had smuggled into the country from Viet Nam.

Bill and I spent considerable time together and

developed a close friendship. We began excursions to pick up girls. We cruised shopping centers, rock concerts, drive-ins—any place we could find females.

"Hey! You chicks wanna smoke a joint?" we would call to alluring girls. Nine out of ten would say "Okay," and we would score.

Our conquests were so successful and our drug-dealing so lucrative, we decided to move in together. My parents supported the idea, hoping the responsibility of having my own place would slow me down. We moved into a house and immediately began to party.

The next night, Bill and I met two pick-ups and were about to take them to our place when we were pulled over by a patrolman.

"Here we go again!" said Bill. "It's Davis, the pig who arrested me in the park for possession."

The officer approached the driver's window cautiously. "Let me see your license," he ordered. "Take it out of your wallet. Get out of the car, Bruce. I want to look in your trunk."

The patrolman examined the trunk, then searched the inside of my car. He didn't find much because I had learned to carry my drugs inside the air filter or taped beneath the engine.

"What are these?" he questioned, pointing to some seeds.

"I don't know," I answered casually. "Looks like birdseed to me."

"Come on, Danzara. You know those are marijuana seeds."

"What right do you have to pull us over, you pig!" Bill exploded from the back seat of my car. "We haven't done anything wrong. Are you trying to rip me off again? You hold us here any longer and I'm gonna bring a lawsuit for police harassment!" he threatened.

"Cool it, Nam, cool it," I cautioned.

"Bill," the officer began with firmness in his voice, "I know what you're doing, and I'm going to get you. I'm going to see you spend the rest of your life in prison. That's a promise!"

Davis pulled me aside.

"Look, Bruce, I don't know how deeply you're tied in with Bill, but let me tell you, he's not the friend you think he is. He's going to end up in prison, and if you hang around with him, you'll end up there, too."

Davis gave me permission to get back into my car. As I did so, he spotted the younger chick sitting in the front seat.

"How old are you, miss? he quizzed.

"Sixteen," she replied demurely.

"It's ten o'clock. Take her home right now, Bruce."

I started the engine and we pulled away. The police car followed us. When we rounded the corner leading to the girl's house, the patrol car was temporarily out of view. Quickly I jumped out of the car and opened the trunk. The girl climbed in, and I closed the lid. Hopping into the front seat just as Officer Davis rounded the corner, it appeared the girl had gone into the house as commanded. The police car did not follow, so we went to our place as planned.

Our new living quarters provided many opportunities to sell large quantities of drugs, but we were next door to a church. When they realized what we were doing, they called the police. A number of patrol cars appeared in the street and after three days, we were evicted.

I moved home, and we started searching again. Brian decided he would join us, so all three of us hunted around town. Finally we spotted a run-down house next to a realty. We could rent it for $100 a month.

As I was moving my stuff out of my parent's house, my dad suddenly had a change of heart. "Bruce," he pleaded, "don't go. Stay here. I'm afraid if you go something is going to happen to you."

"Don't worry, Dad. I can take care of myself. Nothing is gonna happen to me."

Bill and I set up residence right away. After three days, I was busted for selling opium. Somehow my father's premonition had been correct.

Chapter Four
Judgment Day

The prisoners around me moved listlessly on their bunks. A gray depressive cloud filled our forty-man cell.

"What a cheerless way to spend Christmas!" I complained silently to myself. "I've got to get out of here before I snap." At twenty-one years of age, I was not excited at the prospect of spending the next five years in jail.

A voice came over the PA. "The following prisoners have visitors . . ." Several names echoed through the cell. ". . . Bruce Danzara. . . ."

"I wonder who has come to see me." Any visitor would be a welcome relief from the boredom.

Stepping into the visiting room, I was confronted by Nam's smiling face. He was a little high.

"Bill, what are you doing here?" I whispered. "You took a big chance."

"I stick with my friends. How are they treating you?"

"Okay I guess. It's just boring. Life's a drag without drugs."

"Listen man, I'm selling our dope to get money for a good lawyer. I'll get you out. You won't have to go to prison."

"Be careful. They're looking for you. They told me I just got in the way. You're the one they want. They're after you for selling at the park. That guy Officer Davis arrested you with was a narc. He's the one who busted me."

"Man, I'm innocent. They're trying to frame me. I didn't sell to any narc. They're trying to rip me off. Hey, I'll come to the court and slip you a joint."

"Be careful. They'll be looking for you."

"I won't get caught, man. Take it easy. I'll see you later."

I was taken back to my gloomy cell. Apprehension flooded my mind about Bill coming to court.

Four days after our bust, Jeff and I were arraigned. The guards shackled us into a line of fifty prisoners and we were escorted to a bus with barred windows. They transported us to the district courthouse in Westminster.

Through a maze of corridors and cells beneath the courthouse, we were deposited in a large open cell covered like a birdcage. Our handcuffs were removed and sack lunches were presented to us.

The cell was cold. We had no coats, and the chilly cement benches provided little solace. For six hours we shivered, doing our best to stay in a comfortable position. At last we were brought up into the courthouse with several other prisoners.

After spending four days in the concrete and iron-bar jungle, the return to the real world impressed me. People stared as we entered the courtroom, and I began to feel like a hardened criminal. I became painfully aware of my unkempt appearance. I had not been able to shave, and my hair was messed up.

Sharon, my parents, and several of my friends were already in the courtroom. Sharon's face was red and tearstained. Her expression communicated her fear that I would be in prison the rest of my life. My parents stared awkwardly at the floor.

The judge, the district attorney, and several police officers glowered intently as each of the prisoners came in. We were seated in a box, like a jury box, in the left front section of the room. The scene reminded me of a television program.

Sitting in the prisoner's box gave me a good opportunity to survey the courtroom. On the far side, with some of our friends, sat Nam. As I glanced at him, he nodded, then flashed a large cigar-sized marijuana joint, called a bomber.

Officer Davis, who had harassed Bill and me was also sitting in the spectators' section. As he had nothing to do with this case I wondered why he was present. He had a disappointed look on his face, and when I caught his eye, he shook his head slowly in exasperation.

After a few preliminary remarks from the judge, the roll call began. Each prisoner heard the charges against him and was asked to offer his initial plea of guilt or innocence.

It was difficult to keep my mind on the proceedings. I knew Bill was going to attempt to pass the joint to me. I was also aware that people in the room knew Nam by sight. Somehow I had to warn him not to pass it.

Suddenly one of the officers in the front half of the courtroom stood and pointed at Bill. As he pointed, everyone in the room looked in that direction.

"You! Come here!" the officer commanded, motioning with his finger.

Bill stood and began to back away. Suddenly he took the bomber, and right in front of everyone, crammed it into his mouth and dashed toward the door.

Everything exploded. Several spectators leaped up. Three plainclothes officers seized Bill in the aisle and wrestled him to the floor. Nam struggled in vain. Several hands forced his mouth open and someone reached in to retrieve the marijuana. In an instant they were holding his squirming body by the ankles shaking him like a saltshaker in an attempt to dislodge the drug from his throat. He coughed and sputtered, but somehow managed to keep it down. They half-carried, half-dragged him from the courtroom.

A wave of gloom swept over me. The whole world

was against me. Nam's arrest seemed like the beginning of the end; it was an omen of personal disaster. I was certain to face a long prison term.

In a few minutes the excitement died, and the roll call began again.

"Not guilty," I said when the charges against me were read.

"Do you have a lawyer or money to retain the services of a lawyer?" they asked.

"No, I don't."

"Would you like a public defender at the State's expense?"

"Yes, I would."

"Step over here and sign this paper."

Jeff and I were assigned the same public defender. While we talked to him, one of the narcotics officers who had arrested us swaggered up and addressed me.

"You think you're really funny, huh? Trying to make us look like fools, aren't you?" He strode off.

"What does he mean?" I quizzed the public defender.

"The lab report revealed the drug you were selling wasn't opium," he answered.

"I told you it wasn't opium," Jeff offered triumphantly.

"That's good to hear," I replied, a little relieved.

"Yes, but even though it wasn't opium, the charge for bogus sales is the same. But don't worry, in a situation like this, they will probably just make a deal with us. Play it cool. Don't get angry, and don't fly off the handle."

Bail was set at $10,000. My parents didn't have

that kind of cash, but the public defender told me that at the next court appearance, the judge would reduce the bail.

We were taken back downstairs to the birdcage. Nam was sitting red-faced with uncontrollable defiance in his eyes.

"Man, they got you," I attempted to console him.

"This thing's a frame!" he bawled out loudly. "I'm innocent!" he bellowed, smashing his shoes onto the concrete floor as if to punctuate his anger. "They're ripping me off again. I didn't do anything."

Bill was in such a rage, I couldn't keep from laughing. He looked so funny throwing his clothes all over the place so the guards could search him.

On the day before Christmas we appeared in court again and our bail was reduced to $2500 each. My parents told me they would contact a bail bondsman and bring me home that night.

As I sat in our cell waiting to be released, I saw a pathetic sight. A number of men, in jail on trivial charges, were sobbing loudly. It was Christmas Eve and they longed to be home with their families. My parents finally arrived with my bail.

Freedom tasted good. That evening we celebrated Christmas in front of a glowing fireplace. As we opened presents, Sharon clung tightly to my waist and tearfully affirmed her affection. Her devotion and sympathy helped increase my self-pity.

Two days after Christmas, I stepped into my living room to find a former high school English teacher tutoring my sister.

"Oh hi, Mrs. Birchfield."

"How are you, Bruce?"

"Not too good. The police are trying to frame me. The narcotics officers asked me where a friend of mine lived. I didn't know they wanted to buy drugs. All I did was take them to a friend's house. They're trying to make it look like I was trying to sell drugs. They're trying to rip me off. I was just trying to do good to people, like Jesus."

"You're sick, Bruce! You need to see a doctor." Her words startled me. "I'm not sick, I'm perfectly normal. I'm just upset. If you were being arrested unjustly, you'd be upset, too."

"Bruce, I'm a psychologist. You are having severe mental problems. Bruce, you need help. You need to see a doctor."

"I don't need to see a doctor," I retorted defensively.

"What can I do to help you then?"

"Why don't you pray for me?" I challenged in a mocking voice.

Without hesitation she bowed her head and began to pray out loud. Numbed by her reaction to my sarcasm, I looked at the floor. Before Mrs. Birchfield had finished her prayer, she started to cry. She jumped up and left the room. I didn't see her again, but her words haunted me.

Although I had warped the truth, I knew my survival depended on my story. "I'm not crazy; I'm just scared. I have to tell people this story for my protection."

Returning to the house where Bill and I had been living, I discovered our possessions had been stolen. I needed money for a lawyer, so I began to deal heavily in drugs again. This time I was careful to sell only to long-time friends—kids who couldn't possibly be narcotics officers.

My trial was approaching, and I knew Nam would appear at his arraignment on the same date. Somehow, I had to smuggle drugs to him. He had been caught because of me, and I had to do something for him.

The night before my trial I purchased three packages of cigarettes and spent an hour carefully unwrapping the clear plastic wrapper on the bottom of one pack. With the paper exposed, I used a pair of tweezers to pull open the end of the package. I removed several cigarettes and stuffed the package with a number of potent drugs. Nam could get loaded for weeks. When the weight and thickness of the container appeared normal, I sealed the package up with clear glue.

I appeared in court the next day with a couple of girl friends. My parents did not come this time. Bill and Jeff arrived in their blue jail clothes. No one had offered to put up bail for them.

The public defender told us, as he had predicted earlier, that the district attorney's office was willing to make a deal. "If you plead guilty, they'll let you off with two months in jail."

"I don't want to plead guilty. I'm innocent."

"Look, if you plead innocent, they'll nail you. They'll go out of their way to convict you, and you'll probably get five years."

"Five years!" I thought to myself. "That's a long time. I might be able to beat this thing, but if I lose . . . I'm dead."

"Okay," I said finally. "I'll plead guilty and take the two months."

Jeff decided to do the same thing, but Bill insisted he was innocent and would fight the charges he faced.

"Can I buy some cigarettes for my friends?" I asked the bailiff.

"Sure, Danzara. Go ahead."

I looked back towards one of the girls who had come with me. "Go buy three packs of cigarettes for Bill," I told her. She left the courtroom, although the cigarette packages were already in her purse.

When the judge asked me how I pleaded to the charges, I replied, "Guilty, your Honor." I was instantly convicted.

"I'm suspending your sentence and placing you on summary probation for a period of two years. The terms of your probation are that you serve sixty days in the county jail."

I was beginning to sign the papers which acknowledged my conviction, when my female friend entered the courtroom again. "Here are your cigarettes, Bruce."

I met her at the short wooden railing which divided the courtroom, and took the cigarettes from her hand. Stepping up to the bailiff, I handed him the packs and turned to finish signing the papers. I did not dare look in his direction.

He felt the packages and one compressed easily. "What are you doing, Danzara, trying to pass drugs to your friends?"

My face must have turned red. The judge, the district attorney, and everyone in the courtroom stopped what they were doing and looked at me.

"What have you done, you idiot?" my brain screamed. "Now you're really gonna get five years!"

"Sure, I would do some dumb thing like that," I answered in a mildly sarcastic tone. I was struggling to look cool and untroubled. He looked at me curiously for a long moment, then down at the cigarettes.

He must have reasoned I'd be too stupid to attempt smuggling drugs to my friends in such an obvious way because he handed the packages to Bill. One long, relieved breath flowed from my lungs.

When court was dismissed, I was allowed to go home for three days until my two-month sentence began. My parents quizzed me about the outcome of the trial.

"I have to spend two months in county jail."

"Two months! Didn't you plead innocent?"

"The public defender told me if I pleaded innocent they'd frame me into spending five years in jail."

"He shouldn't have told you that. When you pleaded guilty, you got a felony conviction. Do you know what that will mean the rest of your life? I think you should see if you can change your plea. Why don't you find a good lawyer?"

"Dad's right," I told myself. "I can still beat this thing."

I found a lawyer and told him my story. He claimed he'd do his best for me if I retained him. So I paid him $500.

He telephoned the courthouse and did some quick checking. "They say your case is closed, Bruce. I'm sorry, but there's nothing more I can do for you."

I walked numbly from the lawyer's office. It was the fastest $500 I ever spent.

Chapter Five
Two Months in
County Jail

I had been in jail before, but my destination now was a completely different section of the facility. All kinds of stories are passed around about the main jail. The other prisoners claimed it contained hardened criminals convicted of heinous crimes. I was to be confronted by this unknown world, but what bummed me out most was the thought of two months without dope.

The morning before entering jail, I ran around town with Sharon accumulating a supply of potent drugs. I collected hashish, acid, a few reds, and some other barbiturates. I condensed the drugs tightly in a balloon, which I tied off and put into my pocket.

Sharon and my parents drove me to the jail. Shortly before noon, I visited the rest room and plopped the balloon into my mouth. When I attempted to swallow, it stuck in my throat and for one long moment I gagged. Finally it slipped into my stomach.

At noon I kissed Sharon and my parents good-bye and pressed the button at the jail door. "Yes?" an officer answered through the intercom.

"I'm here to turn myself in." The buzzer sounded and I opened the door.

The guards searched my thoroughly. They took my fingerprints, then gave me two free phone calls. I took a shower, was sprayed with insecticide, then received my blue jail uniform. I feared they would take an X-ray and discover the drugs in my stomach, but none was taken.

When the processing was completed, I was led through a long series of iron bar doors and placed in an eight-man cell. I quietly took my bunk and carefully eyed each man in the small cell.

I was in O tank, where all the drug offenders, bikers, and the fighting types are put. Almost everyone in O tank had refused work detail. Upstairs was P tank where the prisoners who had agreed to work were housed. They had televisions and playing cards.

One of my cellmates was called Rusty. He was about five feet eleven inches tall and weighed 250 pounds. Deacon, another prisoner, had been convicted of armed robbery and sodomy. He had been in this same cell for eight months, and his skin was starting to scale.

Deacon and Rusty were the hard guys of O tank. They were feared by almost everyone and were considered leaders of the cellblock. I became friends quickly with these men, wanting them on my side in case any trouble broke out.

Larry, another cellmate, had a full beard and hair that reached the center of his back. I thought he looked like Jesus Christ. Larry knew a lot of my friends in the drug group called the brotherhood.

Our cell scarcely had room for its eight occupants. Two sets of bunkbeds were on both sides with a small toilet at one end. There was barely enough room to walk between the beds.

Adjoining our cell was a compartment called a day room. Smaller, it contained a shower and one tiny table on which we could write letters. The door leading into this cubicle was opened for only four or five hours each day.

Food in jail is not too appetizing. Breakfast and dinner were filling meals, but lunch was a waste of time. We had names for many of the delightful dishes we were served. There was "red death" which looked like pink hash browns, and "SOS" which was chipped beef on toast.

Only spoons were entrusted to us for our rations. Because of riot danger, we all sat and stood on command. When meal time was over, regardless of whether we had finished eating, we were commanded to stand and leave the mess hall together. Everyone devoured his food with haste to avoid going away hungry.

There were a number of vegetarians in jail. At dinner I tried my best to sit near one of them. They would trade their meat for my over-cooked vegetables or some dish I didn't care for.

After three days in jail, I finally had a bowel movement and recovered my drugs. At first, no one knew of them, but I decided to turn Larry on because he was cool. It didn't take long for everyone to discover the two of us had dropped acid. When they found out, I had to share my drugs with everyone, and everything was quickly used up. Psychologically I depended on marijuana, and with none to be had, I became irritable and tense.

"Danzara," a guard quizzed one day, "you want

to go to a work farm? You'll get five days dropped off your sentence for each month you work."

"Yeah, I want to work." The extra time off would make it worthwhile.

"You'll have to get your hair cut."

"Why? What difference does it make if my hair is long or short?"

"Regulations. You'll have to cut it to work."

I wanted to get into the sun and work, but had no desire to cut my hair. It was the principle, and my cellmates encouraged me to stay in the main jail.

"Stay in here, man. O tank is better than the work farm. Besides, everybody is cool in here." Because I would not go to the barber, I never saw the farm.

We were in cell number one, closest to the guard's house. We often warned the rest of the cellblock when a guard was coming. We'd make a certain whistle or animal call to signal his presence.

At night no one could sleep because of heat. The cellblock often erupted into a variety of jungle sounds. All evening prisoners mimicked animal noises until you literally felt you were in a zoo. It was difficult to obtain even four or five hours of sleep a day.

Jail is a mini-community. Every crime inflicted in the street is committed in jail. Rape, murder, muggings, and thefts all take place. I witnessed many different crimes.

It didn't take long to realize most prisoners agitate for fights to vent their frustrations. Because loners are easily picked on, it is best to have friends. I was fortunate my cell mates were tough. They would come to my aid if needed.

I also discovered those who returned from meals

early have opportunities to rob other prisoners. Men have been killed over candy bars, so I was careful to come back last from chow. I avoided any situation which might provoke a fight.

With little to take up our time we spent many hours talking. One day the subject of our conversation turned to men from India who eat glass.

"That's nothing," Rusty volunteered. "I eat razor blades."

"Sure, man," someone mocked him, and everybody laughed.

"No, really, give me a fresh pack of razor blades and I'll show you."

Someone handed him a fresh package from the sink, but our cell was full of disbelievers.

"Really, you guys, I eat them all the time."

Rusty unwrapped the package and took out a new blade. He split the steel lengthwise with his fingers, then placed one piece between his teeth on the left side of his jaw and the other piece on the right side. He closed his mouth with one grating "crunch!"

The rest of us looked on in amazement as Rusty casually chewed away. I expected him to spit blood at any moment, but after twenty crunches he swallowed his metalic meal.

"The secret is to keep the blades on your teeth," Rusty intoned matter-of-factly. "Here, I'll eat some more."

We all sat in disbelief as this idiot systematically consumed three more fresh blades. We all expected him to keel over from a hidden cut somewhere deep in his body, but although he picked a few small steel slivers from his teeth, he seemed to suffer no ill effects.

After a month in O tank, rumors claimed the jail was going to be reorganized, and we would be moved to another module in the building. We were going to be divided into two groups, one would go to six-man cells downstairs, while the other section would be assigned to four-man cells upstairs. No one desired to go up, because the cells were smaller, and heat would rise into them. I was dejected upon hearing I had been assigned an upper cell.

My new home contained three unfamiliar faces. Two of my new companions were white, but the other was a black named Harris. Harris was the only Negro in our cellblock. He was six feet eight inches tall and had only one eye. He never said anything; he just stared with that eye.

Because blacks were not appreciated in the predominately white Orange County Jail, word spread through the cellblock that Harris was going to be killed. The prisoners began to call him names and for two solid days they taunted and threatened him.

I was worried he might kill one of us to scare everyone else. Harris had a razor blade which was stuck into the end of a pencil, to make a small knife. He always kept it up and ready. The three of us began to sleep in shifts so someone would always be awake and ready to warn the others in case Harris attacked in the middle of the night.

After lunch one day, a dozen white prisoners advanced menacingly up to our cell door. They were all holding weapons of some kind and they closed in on Harris.

"You'd better get out of here, man. We don't want blacks in here. If you don't leave, we're gonna kill you."

"Yeah?" Harris snarled back defiantly. "You whiteys may get me, but I'll take three of you with me."

Right then the guards came, and all the prisoners rushed back to their cells. Harris jumped up and ran into the corridor.

"You're not keeping me in here!" he yelled to a black guard.

"You ain't going no place," the guard yelled back.

"I'm leaving here, man. I ain't gettin' killed by no crazy white boys."

When the guard realized what was happening, he had Harris moved to another section of the jail.

The prisoner who replaced Harris offered little relief. He was a middle-aged man accused of manslaughter. He admitted slaying his wife and was suffering from tremendous guilt. He gazed blankly at the ceiling all day with wildly dilating eyes. He looked insane.

We tried to be friendly, but every time we started to talk to him, he backed up like a cornered animal.

"I know you hippies are going to try to kill me," he would shriek. "I'll murder you if you try! I murdered my wife, and I'll murder you too!"

Because he had killed once and was obviously quite paranoid, we decided not to take chances. We went back to sleeping in shifts.

Everyday I received a new letter from Sharon, but she never visited. I decided I would drop her when my sentence was finished. I was suffering from loneliness and yearned to be free. I felt like crying. Jail was a nightmare that simply would not end.

In the cell next to mine was a fellow called Red. He was friends with the hard guys in our block including my ex-cellmates.

An old friend of Red's was placed in a six-man cell on the bottom level. Red immediately accused the newcomer of turning him in to the police.

"Man, you informed on me to the pigs." Calling to his friends he cried, "This is the guy who turned me in. He's the reason I'm in here right now."

"I didn't snitch on you, Red," the man replied defensively. "Why are you telling everybody that? You know that's not true."

"Informer" is the worst charge one prisoner can level against another. It is like passing a death sentence. Red kept up his verbal barrage until several prisoners began to breathe out threats of their own to the so-called informer.

One day after a meal, several thugs vaulted down to the next level and attacked him. Although I couldn't see his cell, the reflection of what was happening could be seen in the bullet-proof glass separating us from the next section.

The wretched fellow was screaming for the guards while attempting to kick his attackers away from his bunk. They managed to seize his legs and drag his flailing body out of the cell. They struck him mercilessly.

"Isn't this neat?" one of my cellmates breathed excitedly.

"I think it's perverted," I answered.

They crushed his ribs and skull with their shoes, and the man's torso went limp.

"For God's sake, stop!" another prisoner shrieked from our level.

One of the attackers checked the victim's heart beat.

"His heart stopped!" he cried, and all the murderers quickly scaled back up the bars to their cells.

"Don't nobody talk!" bellowed one of the attackers.

"Shut up! Anybody talks and we'll kill em!" threatened another.

In moments the guards found the man's crushed body and called for the medic. They quickly administered oxygen, then carried him off.

"All right, who did this?" the guards demanded.

"We didn't see nothing. What happened?"

"What are you talking about?"

No one told. Every prisoner was afraid he would be next. The strong and crazy people ruled. After the guards left, I couldn't contain myself any longer. Even though my opinion was unpopular, I had to voice it.

"No one knows that guy really did anything wrong. Everybody's always talking about injustices in here—man, that guy didn't even get a trial. They killed him just because one man said so."

Jail was beyond my comprehension of how bad living conditions could get. I had no idea violence went unchecked. The unbelievable perversion made me sick to my stomach. I began to dream of release day.

When Dad came to visit me, I begged him to get me out. "I'm willing to do anything to get released early. Talk to the judge. Tell him I want to go to college for the spring semester. I've got to get released."

My father sought out the judge who had sentenced me and convinced him to let me out of jail nine days early to attend college. I was released immediately. The relief I experienced was overwhelming. That first joint tasted very good.

Although my confinement had been for less than two months, I found great difficulty adjusting to the normal world. At home, I instinctively gulped down my mother's meals. On campus to register for classes, I felt uneasy talking to girls. It was difficult to get back into the swing of things.

The terms for my early release stated I would be a full-time student and earn money at a part-time job. After several weeks of school, I was to appear before the judge with a work record and proof of college enrollment. The judge let me off on the condition I serve my remaining nine days over Easter vacation.

I had not gotten a job and feared the judge would give me a longer sentence. The day before my court appearance, I purchased a receipt book and forged several sales slips to make it appear I had worked as a landscaper and painter. When the judge saw the receipts he was pleased.

I determined to smuggle more drugs into jail. I placed a good supply in a baggy, tied it off, and pushed it down my throat. Once I had swallowed it, I wondered if I had tied it off carefully enough.

After entering jail again, I became constipated. For several days I broke into a cold sweat, imagining that the baggy had come undone and the drugs were being absorbed into my system. If that happened, I would overdose and might die.

After five days, I had my first bowel movement and recovered the drugs. I got loaded immediately. Stashing the drugs in my bed, I put one pill in my pocket and went to lunch. When we returned from the mess hall, the guards were in the middle of a shake-down inspection. They were examining every bunk.

I started to shake. They found my drugs. "I'm busted for sure! I shouldn't have brought them in!" Quickly I took the pill from my pocket and stepped on it. The guards pulled me aside and searched me.

"Where did you get those drugs, Danzara?"

"What drugs? How could I get drugs in here? That's the last thing I'd do. I just got busted for drugs, why would I do a stupid thing like bring more drugs in here?"

They seemed to accept my story, but I kept expecting to be rebooked for illegal possession of drugs. Fortunately, no new charges were brought.

On Easter Sunday morning I was released from jail. I looked back at the building and told myself, "Never again. I'm never going to come back here—never!"

Two days later I walked into a doughnut shop with three girls to see Jeannie, Nam's girl friend before he was arrested. Bill had been convicted and was serving a five-year sentence. I was a little high on a joint and two glasses of wine which I had earlier in the evening, but felt confident I could maintain sobriety in public. Two highway patrolmen sitting in the doughnut shop watched us as we came in.

"Hi Jeannie. How are you?"

"I'm pretty good. Hey Bruce, would you do me a favor?"

"Sure, what is it?"

"My car ran out of gas and I left it over near Disneyland. Would you mind getting it for me?"

"Sure, Jeannie. No problem."

We left the doughnut stand for her car. I looked up in my rearview mirror to see we were being red-lighted. "Don't worry," I told the girls calmly. "It's probably just for my taillight."

I pulled over right in front of a highway patrol station. When I stepped out of my car, the officer threw me against his patrol car and shook me down for drugs. The girls were ordered out of the car, and they searched it for drugs.

"What are you loaded on?" the officer quizzed me.

"I'm not loaded."

"Look at the badge on my cap," the policeman commanded, shining his flashlight into my eyes. "Let me see your teeth." I opened my mouth and he scraped my teeth looking for some kind of drug fragment. "Breathe in my face," he commanded, and when I did he announced, "You're drunk." He made me walk a straight line and touch a finger to my nose; both of which I was able to do without problems.

The trunk of my car, which had been searched many times, somehow produced a baggy full of moldy marijuana stems. The eyes of the policemen grew big. They placed a match under the stems.

"Ah ha! Marijuana!" they howled at the odor.

By now there were four police cars parked around mine. Every patrol car coming in or out of the station stopped to see what was happening.

"We're placing you under arrest for possession of marijuana, being under the influence of alcohol, drunk driving, and contributing to the delinquency of minors."

"Look, I just got out of jail. I'm not loaded, and I

haven't done anything wrong. Give me a break, will you?"

They called a sergeant over to talk to me. I told him my situation. "Please give me another chance. I'm going to school to become a teacher. I've served my time, and I just want to have another chance in life."

I had instructed the girls to cry and do anything that could get us off. Out of the corner of my ear I could hear one of them say, "You cops are a bunch of pigs. He hasn't done anything wrong." Then she spewed forth profanity. I had just finished telling the sergeant how nice the girls were when she started swearing.

"Is that how nice girls talk? They don't sound so sweet to me."

"Just a minute," cried the officer who had pulled me over. He swaggered over to my car dramatically, leaned into the back seat, and pulled out a red. "Seconal!" he said sarcastically. "You're busted!"

My car had been searched for twenty minutes. I was certain he had planted the capsule, but there was nothing I could do. They handcuffed me and took all of us to the Orange County Jail.

"Wow, I'm going to cut my hair this time," I thought. "I'm gonna do anything I can to get out early." They gave me two phone calls, so I telephoned my parents. When Dad heard I was in jail again, he started to cry. He was crushed.

They placed me in the drunk tank with the alcoholics. Although my head was clear, I stayed in it for seven hours. It wasn't until 6 A.M. the next morning that I was placed in a regular cell. Several prisoners who had seen me in jail two days earlier were surprised to see me again.

"What happened to you? Weren't you just released?"

"They busted me again—on worse charges."

As I lay back on my bunk, I cried to God in my heart. "Please don't let me go to prison. I'll do anything to get out of jail. I'll be a good person from now on. Please God. You're the only one who can help me."

"Danzara," the guard called. "Roll it up."

"Wow, what's happening?" I thought to myself. "Am I going to court? Maybe I got bailed out."

"You're being released. The highway patrol didn't file charges."

Chapter Six
Tripping Out

When summer arrived, I became reacquainted with an old high school buddy named Ron. Nothing exciting was happening in Garden Grove, so we decided to travel north. Neither of us had ever seen Haight-Ashbury in San Francisco, so that became our goal. As we had only $5 between us, we decided to try hitchhiking.

Traveling slowly up the coast, we could catch only short rides, and it seemed we were always deposited at lonely off-ramps where few cars entered the freeway. We had to wait hours for each lift and we reached San Francisco after two sleepless days. The sun was setting as we arrived at the intersection of Haight and Ashbury streets.

We had both envisioned the district as free-and-easy with many colorful psychedelic signs. We were stunned by the sight of a depressing slum. Almost all the girls on the street appeared to be prostitutes; the good looking females ran when we tried to speak to them. Many of the men looked as if they would kill us for a fix; some were obviously trembling from heroin addiction. As it grew dark, everyone began to desert the streets.

The weather had been beautiful up the coast, but now it was turning cold. Ron and I were both wearing short-sleeved shirts, and neither of us was prepared for a chilly night.

"We'd better find a place to crash, fast," Ron declared.

We had heard of a program which assisted people in finding temporary lodging. We made our way to its headquarters. There were Christian pictures on the walls.

Twenty other vagrants were also waiting for places to sleep. The director answered telephone calls from people with spare rooms. After each call, he dispatched several migrants to fill the vacancy.

I lit a cigarette and the director scowled in my direction. "There's no smoking in here. Put that out right now!"

"What's this guy's trip," I thought exasperatedly. "If we didn't need lodging so badly, I'd tell him off."

At 9 P.M., Ron and I were finally directed to a place on Franklin Street where we would spend the night. We were standing on the curb wondering how to find the street when a cab pulled up.

"Hop in, you guys," said the young cabby. "I'll

take you wherever you want to go. I'm not gonna get customers this time of night anyway."

"Gee, thanks."

When we arrived at the Franklin Street address, the driver cautioned us. "I'd be careful if I were you. Lots of alcoholics hang around here, and it's easy to get ripped off."

As he drove away we took a closer look. All the buildings were run down. Several drunks were lying in nearby alleys, and one suddenly moaned and knocked over a bottle.

"Another *great* neighborhood."

"Man, I'm too tired to worry about it now," Ron replied. "Let's give this place a try." He knocked on the door.

"Oh, you must be the fellows they called me about. Come in. My name is Eric."

Ron and I looked at each other. The man's manner seemed to indicate he was a homosexual. But we were too tired and hungry to worry. We entered the house and our host led us into a back room.

"You can sleep here if you want."

The look on Ron's face betrayed his reluctance to crash while our host was around. We began to talk hoping he would tire and leave the room.

"Hey, would you boys like some wine?" he asked.

"That sounds great."

We began to drink, not thinking we hadn't had anything to eat all day. The wine quickly went through our empty stomachs. Our heads began to spin and our eyes turned bright red.

After a knock at the front door, our host returned

with a male friend. We quickly realized he was Eric's boyfriend. The four of us became enmeshed in a discussion centering on religion and drugs. Eric kept turning the conversation to homosexuality, but Ron and I kept changing the subject.

Soon three more men arrived. Although I couldn't tell if they were straight, I was beginning to feel outnumbered. One of the visitors was a black drummer for a popular rock group. He looked normal to me.

"Hey, it's awfully crowded here," the black suggested to Ron. "If you want to crash at my pad you're welcome."

"Far out," Ron replied, "I'll be right with you."

I couldn't believe my ears.

"What are you doing?" my brain screamed. I tried to convey my feelings by the expression on my face, but Ron didn't notice. In a moment, I was alone with my effeminate host and his friends.

"If you're tired, Bruce, why don't you go to bed. It's my bed, so it's okay."

"Oh no," I lied, "the conversation's really interesting."

By now it was difficult to keep my eyes open. I was determined not to fall asleep while these strangers sat around. Two more of the group left, leaving the owner and his boyfriend.

The conversation kept coming back to homosexuality. Each time my host made a point for his position, he added, "Of course you know what I mean, don't you, Bruce?"

Eric's boyfriend began to argue with him. Apparently he was becoming jealous of me. This situation continued for over an hour, until the phone rang. Eric answered it.

"You're kidding! Oh, that's too bad! Okay . . . yes . . . no problem. Everything's cool."

Our conversation started again, but was quickly interrupted by a loud banging noise outside. The two men checked on the noise, but when they came back, Eric announced, "It's just the neighborhood we live in."

We tried to continue our conversation but the thumping sounds were too distracting. "What *is* that noise?" I demanded.

"I can't keep it from you any longer," Eric's boyfriend confessed. "It's your buddy. He's outside and he wants you. He got in trouble at our friend's house."

"I'll be seeing you guys," I responded promptly.

"Bruce, don't leave," Eric pleaded.

"Look man, that's my friend out there. I came with him and I'm going with him."

"Bruce, if you stay here with me I'll give you anything."

"What do you mean?" cried the boyfriend jealously.

"Bruce, please stay."

"No way, man. I'm leaving."

I came to the front of the house where Ron was thrashing on the door and screaming for me. When I threw open the door, he jumped back with his fists up. He was freaked out.

"Ron, it's me!"

"Bruce! Let's get out of here."

"I'm with you!"

We started to run. When we were a block away, the gays began to chase us on foot, but we had a long lead and they quickly gave up. When we stopped running I asked Ron what happened.

"That guy made a pass at me! I got so scared I hit him and knocked him out cold!"

"He must have called Eric after you split."

"That situation was weird!"

"What are we gonna do now? We're never gonna find a place to stay at this hour."

"I know," Ron suggested, "Let's find a cop and turn ourselves in. We can spend the night in jail."

For half an hour we searched until we finally found a policeman. Obviously high from the wine, our eyes were bloodshot and we could barely maintain balance.

"Book us, we're drunk." We told the cop what had happened and said we wanted to sleep in jail.

"Yeah, I know how things are around here, but you guys haven't committed a crime, have you?"

"Well no, but can't we just spend the night in jail?"

"I can't let you do that. Look, why don't you go over to that on-ramp and hitch a ride. That will take you south towards LA."

No matter how we argued, the officer wouldn't arrest us. Finally we decided to take his advice. Exhausted, we mounted the on-ramp and started thumbing. It was 1 A.M. and few cars were passing. For two-and-a-half hours we shivered in the freezing night and tried to flag a ride to anywhere.

At 3:30 a car pulled up and the driver offered a lift to San Jose.

"Outa sight. That's where we want to go."

We couldn't remember where San Jose was in relation to San Francisco, but it was away from where we were now, and anything had to be better than this cold, unfriendly city.

We hadn't gone far when the driver said, "This is where I turn off. You'll probably want to stay here on the main highway."

As he pulled away, we realized we were a long way from San Jose. It was pitch black. We couldn't even see our hands in front of our faces. The morning cold began to torture us again. It was four o'clock and an icy wind cut into our bodies, making them tremble. We knew our skin was turning purple.

To make our situation even more intolerable, few cars were passing. When an auto did drive by, the darkness hid our presence until the vehicle was almost past.

In the quiet morning our chattering teeth suddenly became comical. Our situation had become so pathetic we had to laugh to maintain sanity. Abruptly our laughter turned to cursing. We cursed San Francisco, the cars that would not stop, and our own faulty judgment.

"Whose idea was this trip anyway?" Ron asked.

"I don't know. Jail didn't wipe me out this much. I sure wish we were back in Garden Grove."

My legs began to buckle, so I curled into a ball on the frozen road. I couldn't sleep and the side of my body quickly went numb.

At 5:00, the first signs of dawn appeared on the horizon, but we felt no warmth at all. When the sun finally rose above the hills in the east, warm rays penetrated our skin for the first time. Never had we wanted the sun so badly.

At 7:00, many cars were zooming by, but none would stop. As they passed, we cursed at the drivers. We were tired and frustrated. It seemed we would never escape this dead end.

By 8:00, we were completely thawed out, but still the sun rose, and with it, the temperature. At 10:00 the thermometer stood at 90 degrees. By 11:00, it had reached 100 degrees—and still no ride! It was so hot we began to sway back and forth. The sudden temperature change had made us sick.

We knew why no one would pick us up. We had long hair and looked as if we hadn't had a bath in months. It was a difficult time to hitchhike. Several hitchhikers and drivers had recently been murdered and no one wanted to take chances.

At noon, we were finally given a ride to Salinas. We were dropped off on U.S. Highway 101 in the middle of a farm area. When the nearby field workers saw our long hair and dirty clothes, they began to swear at us in Spanish. Several cars drove by, and the men swore at us in broken English. We became anxious for our safety.

Every time a highway patrol car drove by, we waved frantically for them to pull over. They'd take one look at us, wave back, and keep driving down the road.

A truck went by filled to capacity. The driver yelled, "Can't give you a ride, but here—" and he threw a big marijuana joint to us. We hadn't had any drugs for two days and that joint looked good. We lit up and smoked it by the road.

The next thing I knew, my body was on fire. My face felt as if it were being dipped in hot grease and the skin around my eyes was so puffed-up I could barely see. My head was buzzing.

The joint had caused us to fall asleep under the hot sun for four long hours. We were severely sunburned.

"Man," I told Ron, "I don't know what I look like, but you look bad."

"You look bad too. Your face is as red as a beet."

"If we look this bad now, how are we gonna look in a few more hours?"

We felt as if we had crawled out of the sewer. I could never remember looking this bad before. I couldn't take it any more. I started to pray. We had to get out of this situation, and only God could help.

An old station wagon pulled up with two guys and their girl friends. "We're going to Carmel, that help you any?"

"Man, that's great."

When we got out of their car in Carmel, another car pulled up. "When was the last time you ate?" the driver asked in fatherly tones.

"Three days."

"Get in," he commanded. He immediately drove to a supermarket in Carmel and parked. "Wait right here." He disappeared into the market.

We couldn't believe it. No one else had bothered to help us, and this man didn't even have long hair. He returned with two bags of groceries.

"Here's some food," he announced, and plopped the bags in our laps. "Take this money. Is that enough to buy food until you make it home?"

"Yeah! This is great! We'll have to pay you back."

"No, no, that's okay. I've been in tight situations and somebody helped me. I guess it all equals out."

When he left, we gorged ourselves on the food. We ate big hunks of cheese, bread, and fruit. The ordeal was over. We made it back to Garden Grove the next day.

Chapter Seven
Live And Let Die

I was spending a good deal of my time at a nightclub called Finigan's Rainbow. Many friendly girls hung out at the club, and there was little difficulty getting something going.

One night at the club, I met a Viet Nam veteran named Paul. We went to his place to get loaded. When Paul was high, he poured out his problems.

"I was going to be a minister once," he confessed, "but now I can't forgive myself. I just came back from Nam and I'm all messed up."

"See a lot of action?" I asked.

"Too much. That's the problem. Everybody told me how great it was to fight for your country, but I got all messed up. The first time I killed someone, it shook me up so much I threw up my guts. After that it was easy to kill, and I almost enjoyed it. I can't forget what I did. I'm having nightmares almost every night."

"Don't you know God can forgive you?"

"Yeah, I guess so."

"All you have to do is ask God to forgive you. Don't feel bad about the past. God loves you, and he forgives."

My religious background gave me the right words of cheer, and Paul began to look to me as a spiritual leader. He lived close to Finigan's, so I moved in with him. This gave us both cheaper rent and a good place to bring chicks after an evening at the nightclub. By Christmas, things were getting pretty wild again.

I decided to go to a three-day rock concert given to celebrate Christ's birthday. The festival was located in the Laguna Hills. By the time I arrived with a girl named Sherri, so many people were in attendance, we had to park our car two miles down the road. The police set up roadblocks to keep people out, but the crowds poured over the unguarded hills surrounding the concert site. About 10,000 people were already on the grounds, and by noon 30,000 were walking around. The total attendance was estimated at 50,000.

We walked through the main entrance and spotted a guy holding a giant sucker made of Orange Sunshine, a powerful LSD synthesized by the brotherhood. One lick of that sucker would get you wasted. We saw kids take bites of it.

Sherri and I sat near the platform. Somebody passed us some psychedelics and we helped ourselves. All kinds of drugs were being passed around. Some kids were already so loaded they were running around naked. All types of people were at the festival. The Hare Krishna were passing out literature condemning killing of any kind. Every odd religious group seemed to be present in force.

Several speakers managed to get control of the microphone to preach at us. One claimed Jesus came to show us how to love one another. "Now this is how Christmas ought to be celebrated," I commented to Sherri.

"Jesus took drugs," the speaker continued. "He was the first real hippie. He knew how to get high and how to turn others on."

A guy in front of us jumped to his feet. He was carrying a Bible. "*No!*" he yelled. "You're wrong, you're all wrong! Jesus didn't come to turn you on to drugs. He came to give you life. He said, 'I am the way, the truth, and the life. No man can come to the Father but by me.' Jesus wants to give you eternal life. That's why He came.''

Everyone listened to this Jesus freak. He was standing in front of us and seemed to be looking directly at me. ''Jesus doesn't want you to use drugs! What you're doing is wrong! Jesus is in heaven crying at the way you're living!''

At this statement, the crowd reacted. They booed him down and several in the throng picked him up and pushed him to the side. We didn't see him again, but his message stung my mind, and I had to work at forgetting what he had said.

By now Sherri and I were both beginning to hallucinate. It was different from a normal acid trip; I felt my brain was being shot from a cannon. There had been strychnine in the acid because we were both becoming sick and beginning to shake.

We decided to leave. Walking through the crowd, I saw several of my friends. As I looked at them, their flesh shriveled and bones popped out of their skin. I turned away.

''Come on, Sherri, we have to get out of here.''

When we reached the hilltop overlooking the concert, we were so loaded we sat down to keep from falling. We couldn't walk, so we crawled into a small wash on the other side of the hill. Sherri held me. She was scared. Vomiting relieved our systems of some of the poison.

The stream bed in which we sat was full of small stones exposed by a recent rain. The stones glistened like beautiful gems. We were crawling in a jewel box. Like kids we threw these fabulous stones into the air.

Everything around us was alive and vibrating. We were melting into the earth and the towering trees waved at us. The sky was a deep blue spotted with white fluffy clouds. Letters appeared in the heavens and I arranged them with my imagination to form words.

The sky ripped open as if it were being torn. The daytime blue was brushed aside, and a black night with stars appeared through the tear.

Abruptly a giant hand reached out of the rip. The palm possessed a deep wound, and I knew instantly it was Christ's hand. He was reaching to me saying, "Come to Me." The Jesus freak's words echoed in my brain. My mind rebelled at this hallucination, and I looked away. Sherri and I returned to the festival.

This was the first of many visions I was to have of Christ. In the months ahead, I began to drop more acid in search of deeper religious experiences.

I met a girl named Karen at Finigan's. She was under age but had a false ID. "Hey, ya wanna come over to my place and get loaded?"

"Sure," she cooed. "I'd love to get loaded with you."

I took her to my apartment, and we made love. Later Karen asked for some reds. She was a red freak, and although she was already high, I figured she knew what she was doing. I gave her five capsules. After she swallowed them, she began to cough and fell on her side.

"What's wrong?"

"Oh," she moaned. "I took twenty-three reds tonight."

"Wow. When did you take them?"

"Before I met you," she replied groggily.

In a moment she keeled over. I shook her, but she was unconscious. She felt like a dead fish. Her heart was beating, but only faintly.

"What am I gonna do?" I worried. "She's only fifteen. If she dies on me I'm busted for sure. I've got to get her out of here."

Karen was so limp it was difficult to maneuver her body but somehow I stood her up and dragged her outside to my car. She offered no help at all. I sat her up in the front seat, but her head would not stay erect. It was difficult to keep from panicking. Someone might become suspicious.

I drove back to the nightclub and pulled into the parking lot. Every two minutes a police car cruised the lot. I couldn't decide whether to push her out of the car onto the pavement or try to drag her into the club. If a police car pulled through the lot while I was doing either, I would be arrested for sure.

After debating for several minutes, I decided to take her into the club. I opened Karen's door and stood her up. Putting my arm around her waist, I tried to make it look like she was walking and half dragged her the short distance to the nightclub front door.

Before I reached the door, a patrol car pulled up. Karen began to moan and I could tell the officers were looking at us. Quickly I dragged her into the club and plopped her in a chair.

"Don't leave me," she called out loudly as I started to pull away. She wouldn't let go of my arm and everybody was looking at us. The police were coming in, so I frantically pulled away and ran into the head.

Karen's girl friends came to her and kept her from getting busted. Somehow she survived all those reds. When the police left, I slipped out and went home.

Paul and I decided to throw a giant party at our apartment. We invited all our friends from the nightclubs in the area. We were dealing heavily and had all types of dope in our apartment.

I was drinking a lot of alcohol, and it was no problem for me to polish off a whole bottle of wine. At the party, I downed a half gallon. I quickly started hallucinating, and my vision became obscured.

"Did somebody spike this wine?"

"Yeah," a guy answered. "I put fifty tabs of acid in it so everybody could get high."

"Man, I just drank the whole thing!"

I had received fifty doses of LSD! No wonder I was feeling bad. My body was tense and starting to perspire. Everything was becoming confused and disjointed.

The strange light patterns being thrown from Paul's strobe and the heavy rock music caused my mind to become more and more confused. There was a statue of Christ on our dresser, and I realized its eyes were opened! I blinked and looked again. He was looking right at me! "Wow," I thought, "is this really happening?"

Jesus was talking to me. His lips were moving, but the music was so loud I couldn't hear what he was saying. I tried to hear his words, but there was too much noise.

Outside our apartment came a sudden whirling of helicopter blades. A spotlight flashed through the window and a loudspeaker rang out. "This is an illegal assembly. You are disturbing the peace; you must all disperse."

"The police are outside!" somebody yelled. "There are hundreds of pigs outside!"

Everybody panicked. People ran everywhere trying to dispose of their drugs. Our apartment was filled with dope.

"Here," I said to some guy, "will you flush this marijuana for me?" I was too loaded to try it myself.

He was so scared he didn't know what to do. He took the baggy, dumped it on the floor, and ran out the door. I got down on my knees and tried to scoop it up with my hands, but everything was too blurred. I couldn't tell whether I was picking it up or not. Some girl finally helped me.

The police were arresting everyone outside. People were jumping out windows and trying to run by them. It was a gigantic bust.

"The police are coming in!" somebody screamed.

"We've gotta get rid of these drugs!" Paul yelled.

I staggered into the bathroom and saw the toilet was filled with drugs. It had overflowed and there were pills and baggies of marijuana floating on the floor. Paul was using our plunger trying to get everything down. After fifteen minutes he managed to get the toilet to flush again.

Another fifteen minutes went by while we searched the apartment for the drugs everyone had stashed in their fright. We flushed everything away. The police had still not come into our apartment, so

Paul checked outside and discovered they had gone. The pigs had searched and busted most of our friends as they fled, but then they left.

Paul and I realized we had come very close to getting busted. Having already been in jail, I had no desire to go back. Neither of us wanted any more trouble.

"I used to live in Northern California, out in the country," Paul remarked. "It was really neat. There were no police and no hassles. I'm gonna move away from the city and get back to the country."

"Yeah," I agreed, "that would really be neat to have a ranch in the country."

"Look, I've got a settlement coming from that motorcycle accident; I should be getting a couple thousand. Why don't we look for some place in the country?"

"Far out, man."

Several days later we were skimming the paper and saw an ad about a house for rent in Silverado Canyon. I knew several friends who lived there, and they claimed there was no police department in that area.

We went to look at the place. It was a three-bedroom house at the end of a dead end street. We walked up a dirt road, over a stream, and climbed up some stone steps to reach the front door. It possessed a large patio area surrounded by syca-more trees and an intricately designed picket fence. The house was built next to the side of a hill so it was possible to step from the roof onto the hill. The roof itself was flat and was used as a patio. It was perfect.

The owner wanted $185 a month, so we rented it

and moved in immediately. After living in an apartment in the city, our house in Silverado was quite a change of pace. At first there were no girls around, and we began to crave action. Paul and I were driving home from Finigan's one night when we saw two girls hitchhiking on Coast Highway. I pulled over.

"We're on our way up to Silverado Canyon," Paul told them. "Want to come up with us and get loaded?"

"Sure," one of the girls giggled.

We transported the girls to Silverado, and we all got high and made love that night. They said they were on their own, so we let them live with us. We found out later they were runaways. As long as they did our housework and cooking, we let them live with us for nothing.

Although these girls were available any time, we wanted more action, so we brought other girls in to spend the night. There were always several chicks available.

One night at Finigan's, I met an attractive blond named Christine. I brought her to Silverado, and we spent the night together. The next morning she announced she wanted to move in. She used every trick she could to make me let her stay; finally I consented.

The next thing I knew, Christine had become my steady girl friend. No longer could I bring other girls up to our place. No longer could I do what I wanted with our two housemaids. In fact, a conflict developed between her and them and I knew they would move out when they found another place to stay.

One afternoon I came walking up to the house and everyone met me at the door.

"Maaaannn, weee'rrreeee reeeaally looooaded," they said. Their speech was so drawn out and slurred I could barely understand them.

"What are you guys on? Cannibonal?"

We had a large quantity of THC, which is actually an animal tranquilizer. The drug slows down the body processes and makes speech difficult.

"Yeaaaahh. Doooonn't taaaaake iiiit," they answered.

Laughing at their funny speech, I responded, "It's cool. I don't want to be the only one not loaded."

The drug was on the shelf. I picked up the crystals with two fingers and sniffed them into my nose. The moment I sniffed the THC into my nostrils my nose exploded with fire. I had overdosed. I had taken three times as much of the drug as my friends.

Sitting on the floor, I was high in ten minutes. My speech was coming out very slowly. Lying down I decided to relax and enjoy myself.

Suddenly my mind dropped out of consciousness and I felt my spirit leave my body. I tried to open my eyes but couldn't. I was awake, but had no control of my body.

"I'm dying," I panicked. "I've overdosed on cannibonal, and I'm dying."

My eyes were closed, but I could picture my body lying on the floor. I had heard of astral projection, but had never experienced it. Looking back at my lifeless form, I knew this was the end of my life. My soul had left my body.

"I'm dead. I wonder what will happen to my friends? They'll probably get busted. When the police come into the house, they'll find all the drugs I've hidden.''

When Paul realized my eyes were closed, he began to shake me, but nothing could arouse me. He put his head to my chest. "I can't hear his heart. I don't think he's breathing, either." He put a spoon below my nose, but no mist fogged it.

"I think he's dead."

Everything had become fluid. I felt like water inside of water. I was mixed with liquid color. Suddenly I realized that, although I had died, my mind was still alive. "There *is* life after death!" I had always wondered about heaven and hell—now I knew. "I'm going to heaven!"

I was excited and began to enjoy my trip through watery space. But after twenty-five minutes went by and there was no change, it dawned on me I was stuck somewhere in limbo.

"Oh God, no! This is it. I'm not going to heaven. I'm going to be here for eternity.''

My excitement turned to a nightmare. I was already in hell. I couldn't think of anything more terrible than to stay in this fluid state for all eternity. I was nowhere. I was nothing. I was floating like an amoeba in outer darkness.

"God, please help me! It can't end like this!" My mind was fighting my inevitable destiny. "Don't let me stay like this, God!''

After forty-five minutes my eyes opened. My friends were staring at me.

"Wooooow! Weeee thoooouught yoooouu diiieeeed!'' they said. Their voices sounded distorted. They seemed to be speaking through a funnel.

It took three minutes to move my hand from the floor to my chest. Normal body movements were impossible. I tried to speak, but couldn't. By the time my trip had lasted well over an hour, I was finally able to explain in slurred sounds what had happened. I was certain I had actually died and God had brought me back to life.

For the next few days this brush with eternity made me fearful of taking another drug overdose. But after a few weeks, the fear wore off and my life continued as usual.

Chapter Eight
Runnin' the Border

By the time we moved into Silverado Canyon I had taken over 500 LSD trips. While in the canyon I continued to use the drug heavily.

I became a vegetarian after reading a number of books on nutrition. Starting with an all-rice regimen, I then went to the mucous-free diet. I was attempting to perfect my body and make it pure. My friends and I often fasted for a whole week. We would drop different drugs and talk about Christ. In this way we felt closer to God. We believed in "legalized spiritual discovery" (LSD). Marijuana and acid were like sacraments to us.

Every couple of weeks we drove to remote areas in Santa Barbara County to plant marijuana. We cultivated ground in the center of poison ivy patches so no one would come near. We learned quickly not to plant areas to which cows had access. Apparently the cows liked our weed and they, too, could get stoned. We often found grasshoppers lying on their backs at the foot of our plants.

About this time I met a man who could supply me with large quantities of the psychedelic drugs. Gary lived in Modjeska Canyon and had all kinds of dope. He lived a block from the castle, a sixteen-room building from which the brotherhood supplied him with drugs. The ''brotherhood of eternal love'' was an international dope ring. Their old building was equipped with a lab for making drugs like Orange Sunshine.

Those living in the castle told Gary he could bring me up to get my drugs directly from them. Right before I made my first buy at the castle, the FBI raided the building. They arrested everyone in the place and anyone who had dealings with it. They had tapped the phones, and together with international agents in Switzerland and Afghanistan, they arrested a total of sixty people, including Gary. I almost blew it.

Paul, Christine, and I decided to go north for a quick vacation and an opportunity to sell drugs. I bought $2,000 worth of grass, which weighed twenty pounds. We also took 500 tabs of Orange Sunshine acid, some mescaline, hash, and a few other drugs. We hid everything in my new Datsun.

Driving up the coast, I feared being pulled over by the police. They wouldn't have to search my car, they would only have to smell it, as it reeked of marijuana. Drugs were difficult to obtain in the San Francisco area, and we quickly sold everything to

Paul's friends for three times what it had cost me. I made several thousand dollars' profit.

This was my first enjoyable trip to San Francisco, and we visited all the tourist traps. As we walked down Broadway, we saw a large marquee announcing the opening of *Jesus Christ: Superstar*. There were thousands of people waiting to get in to the show, but a number of Christians were picketing the theater.

"I wonder why Christians are against a movie about Jesus Christ?" I thought to myself.

After a few days, Paul flew home, and Christine and I drove down the coast to Santa Cruz to see a friend named Steve. Together we dropped a tab of mescaline and hiked up a nearby pine-covered mountain.

As we reached the summit, we beheld a beautiful sunset. The ocean and rolling hills looked radiantly beautiful in the sun's red rays. We were peaking on mescaline and this magnificent sight dazzled us all.

The sun was swallowed by the ocean and abruptly it became black around us. There was no light unless we looked straight up at the stars.

"We're never going to make it back to the road," Christine shivered. "Maybe we ought to spend the night here. The car must be five miles away. We'll never find it."

"Have you any idea how cold it gets up here at night?" Steve asked. "We have to hike down to the car."

"How are we going to see?" Christine quivered. I could not tell if her voice was trembling because of fear or of cold.

"I've got some matches," I volunteered. "We can

light them one at a time, then walk as far as we can see.''

''Well . . . okay,'' Christine said reluctantly.

The three of us started down together. I was leading the way, Christine was holding on to my shoulder, and Steve was holding on to her. It was the blind leading the blind. I couldn't see a thing. Each time I lit a match, its light obscured my vision and I could see almost nothing in our path.

I moved carefully, warding off tree branches and inching ahead to avoid stepping off some cliff. We were not on a trail and couldn't be certain we were moving in the right direction. Weird howls and crackling sounds surrounded us, causing Christine to sob on my shoulder. I wondered if we were going to make it.

Suddenly we heard a horrible scream. Steve had fallen down the mountain side. Christine and I froze. From far away we heard Steve's voice. ''Man, I fell!''

''Are you all right?'' I yelled between laughs.

''I think so,'' he called back.

Steve slowly climbed up the side of the mountain. He had suffered only bruises and scratches. We continued our slow descent, but suddenly we heard another blood-curdling scream. Steve had fallen again.

This time Christine and I immediately burst into laughter. It was difficult to believe he had fallen twice. Again he was only bruised, and we waited for him to climb up.

Three hours crawled by. We feared we were walking in circles. We screamed for help as loudly as we could, but heard only the echoes of our own voices. After another long hour, we spotted a dim light flickering in the woods ahead. Excitedly we made our way through the trees to a roaring campfire.

"Are we glad to see you," we told the man sitting at the fire. "We got lost. Have you seen an orange Datsun?"

"Sure," he answered, "right over there on the road."

We couldn't believe our luck. We had come down only a few hundred feet from my car. We stayed in Santa Cruz that night, and the next day Christine and I said good-bye to Steve and drove back to Orange County.

Silverado had become a busy place. Fifteen friends were now living with us. Paul and I had retreated to the canyon to flee civilization and its laws. We planned on isolation—but we had calculated wrong. Our friends envied our freedom and began to crash on our living room floor.

My dealing was supporting everyone. I was paying the rent and all the bills. In addition, I was feeding everyone and providing free drugs, which was a heavy loss of money in itself. I fronted drugs to many of the people in our house. They would sell for me and then return a percentage of their profit. Often someone said they couldn't pay what they owed. They knew I wouldn't force payment and were taking advantage of my easygoing nature. I was slowly losing my patience with these freeloaders.

I began pressuring Paul to get a job. "You've got to do your part to pay the bills, man."

"Okay, okay. I've got an idea that will make big money."

Paul was planning a smuggling scheme with a neighbor named Dick. They had a backer who would put up money for a large purchase of hashish deep in Mexico. They asked me to put in several thousand.

"No way. This thing is too risky. I'll put in $500, but that's all."

As the operation drew close, Paul became impassioned. He began to exercise religiously. He did push-ups and ran up and down the hillside to get in shape. He accumulated back-packing equipment and carefully cleaned and prepared it for the journey south. He was treating the operation like a military expedition.

The plan was to drive deep into Mexico and purchase hashish. They would then drive north and Paul would carry the drugs over the border on his back. He would hike over at some barren spot, then they would meet on the U.S. side, switch cars, and come back separately. When they left they took two cars: my orange Datsun and a new white Cadillac they had rented.

Running the border is not easy. I was leery. However, if everything worked out, I would make good money.

I was coordinator for the project. My job was to sit by the phone and wait for Paul or Dick to call. For three days I stayed near the phone. Finally it rang. Dick was on the other end.

"Man, we blew it! We tried to find Paul, but it was too late. He thinks he's a mile from the border but he's gonna come out right at the border check. He's gonna walk right into the Feds."

"Hey man, cool down. You're not making sense. You get the hash?"

"Yeah, we got it, about fifty pounds' worth. Paul's carrying it on his back, but he's gonna get caught!"

"Now, exactly what happened at the border?"

"We let Paul off so he could carry the dope across the border on foot. We thought we were a mile from the border, but we were five miles away! We were gonna meet him on the U.S. side, but we can't find him anywhere. I'm sure he got caught."

"Play it cool, Dick. Paul knows what he's doing. He'll come out all right. Call the Mexican jail to make sure they haven't picked him up. Give me a ring in a couple of days and I'll let you know if Paul calls."

"Okay . . . but Bruce . . . there's something else you've gotta know."

"What's that?"

"Paul wiped out your car."

"Wiped out my car?! How?"

"He was driving up through Mexico when a big locust hit him in the face. He was on reds and he couldn't control the car. We ran into a telephone pole and knocked off the right fender."

"Man, this is a big deal. Why'd you guys get loaded?"

"We just wanted to have some fun."

"Okay, okay. Just call me in a couple of days. But whatever you do, keep your cool."

The next morning the phone rang again. It was Paul.

"Bruce, I'm out in the middle of the desert! I've walked over a hundred miles! I've got to stop. I can't go any longer."

Paul sounded so weary and demoralized I couldn't

contain my laughter. "Where are you?" I asked between laughs. "Are you on the U.S. side of the border?"

"Yeah, I'm at a place called Gila Bend. I hid the hash beside the road a couple miles back. I can't take it any further. I'm gonna fly back to California. I'll come back next week to get the hash."

"Good idea, just fly back."

"Bruce, Dick really blew it."

"What do you mean?"

"When we were in Mexico he was eating whites and didn't sleep at all. We had a flat, and when a gas station attendant told us we'd have to fix it ourselves, Dick punched him in the mouth. Man, he blew it! The police came up and started searching our car—and the drugs were sitting right there. If I hadn't started to talk to them we would have been busted for sure."

"Where you gonna be when Dick calls?"

"I'll be at the Phoenix airport. He can page me if he wants to."

"Okay, great. I'll see you when you fly in."

Dick telephoned later and I informed him how to contact Paul. They met at the airport and Paul gave directions to where the dope was stashed. Dick went after the hash in the Cadillac and Paul decided to drive my car home.

When Paul arrived, I couldn't believe how my new car looked. The car had body damage everywhere. The tires were all chewed up. The right fender was gone and the door was bashed in. Paul told me the damage had been caused by the gigantic locust. He said it hit like a rock.

Dick didn't show up. After several days, we

telephoned around and discovered he had been arrested. The guy who put up most of the money was furious at Dick. I was out a new car and $500.

Some Christians came up to Silverado and invited us to a Maranatha concert. It was a Christian rock music concert being played at a church in Costa Mesa.

Paul and I considered ourselves Christians. We talked about God all the time and had pictures of Jesus in our living room. We even had Christian bumper stickers on our car.

Paul decided to go to the concert. When he returned, he had a funny look on his face. "I accepted the Lord, Bruce."

"What do you mean you 'accepted the Lord?' "

"I asked Jesus into my life. Bruce, it's really neat. It's different from what you and I have been talking about."

He described the concert and encouraged me to come to the next one in Costa Mesa. "Paul, I don't want to 'get saved.' I'm happy the way I am."

My attitude did not discourage Paul's pursuit of this new religious kick. He began to spend time with those Christians and they began to visit our house regularly.

One night, after I had overdosed on cannibonal, Paul came into the house and started talking to me. When he realized I was loaded, he blew up.

"You're going to destroy your life and you want to ruin everybody else's too. Don't you know the word for 'sorcery' in the Bible is the word for 'drugs?' Bruce, you're messed up by Satan. You're evil! I'm moving out! I want to be a Christian!"

Paul was freaking me out; he was putting me on a

bad trip. I wanted to come down but couldn't. "Paul's my best friend," I worried. "What's he doing to me?"

Almost before I sobered, Paul made good his threat and moved out. I couldn't understand why he had gotten so uptight. Somehow he had become a different person.

I had $8,000 worth of mescaline which I was preparing to sell. After the border fiasco, I was afraid the FBI would show up at the house any moment. I decided to take the drug and hide it in some furniture being stored in our garage. The furniture belonged to the former renters, and if the police ever found the drugs, they couldn't make a conviction stick against me.

When I was away from the house one afternoon, the owners of the furniture arrived unexpectedly and carted away their belongings. My mescaline was gone. I called them on the telephone, but they denied finding any drugs. Every cent I had was gone. Silverado had turned into a bad trip. It was time to leave.

Chapter Nine
Ripped Off

Moving out of the canyon, I dumped Christine and attempted to begin dealing again. I met a black named Rudi who had syndicate contacts. They talked of making a $100,000 deal. I wasn't sure if they really meant business, but they talked as if they knew what they were doing.

"I can get all the drugs you want. Let's do some business together."

After I supplied Rudi and his friends with sizeable batches of mescaline, they asked about large quantities of seconal. I checked my sources and found a guy named Jim who had good connections.

Rudi quickly informed his friends about my contact. He said, "They want to start small by purchasing two kegs for $5,000. If everything goes well, they will buy all the reds you can supply."

Passing the information to my contact, he said he would get the kegs and meet us in a deserted location to make the transaction. The deal would net me a full $1,000 profit, and they would probably give me some reds.

Rudi and I drove to a deserted oil field where we met his friends. Jim drove up in another car. While we waited, he took one of the syndicate men and went to pick up the reds. After two hours, we began to worry something had gone wrong. After another hour, the syndicate man came walking back alone. "We've been ripped off!" he yelled.

They grabbed me and started swearing. "Where'd your friend go, Bruce? You're in this together!"

"I don't know anything, honest. I thought he was cool. Look, I lost money too. If I'd been in on this rip-off, do you think I'd be here now?"

"What's your buddy's last name?"

"I don't know; I met him through a friend."

"You set up a deal with someone you didn't know? We don't like what your buddy did to us. Five thousand dollars is a lot of money, brother. Our friends in LA aren't gonna like this. You better remember who your buddy is, quick.''

"Bruce is cool," Rudi interjected calmly. "I know he wasn't in on this." He turned to me, "but you better help us find this guy."

"Get in the car!" they ordered. "We're gonna get that guy. Where can we find him?"

They kept sticking a gun in my ribs. "Look, I'll help you all you want. But just don't point that gun at me, okay?" Ever since the narcotics officer's gun discharged accidentally, I feared guns.

We went to Brian Young's house.

"Is Jim here?" I asked.

"No, he picked up his stuff this morning and split. He was just crashing here for a couple of days."

"Why didn't you tell me? You guys acted like he was your best friend. He just ripped us off."

"Hey, man, we didn't know he was gonna rip you off."

One of the syndicate men pulled out his gun. "You better be telling the truth, or we'll come back. He ripped us off for $5,000 and we want our money."

"Honest, man, he bought a camper and split this morning."

Someone remembered Jim's last name and where his parents lived, so we drove over to his folks' house. The syndicate men asked Jim's parents where he could be found. When they answered slowly, out came the gun. When the pistol appeared, his parents told a little more—but they probably didn't know too much.

Luckily, my revengeful contacts were finally convinced I had nothing to do with the rip-off and let me go. They chased Jim halfway across the country.

They were able to come up with his camper, but they never saw the rest of their money.

One night I was at Finigan's dancing with a chick named Lola when everything started spinning. I ran for a chair and was trying to steady myself when I began to vomit on the rug. Only a few beers and two reds were causing my problems, but somehow this night the combination was deadly.

The bouncer assured me everything was cool. If I hadn't been such a good customer, he would have tossed me out on my ear. Lola and several other girls washed me down with cold towels, but I quickly passed out.

I awoke in a strange bed. The pictures on the wall revealed I was in someone's house. Lola tiptoed into the room. "How are you, Bruce?" she whispered.

"I'm all right, I guess. Is this your pad? How'd I get here?"

"Some of my friends carried you in. Bruce, you can stay as long as you want."

Lola and I became good friends. The next day I moved in my belongings, including my Jesus posters. Lola's friends did a double take when they saw my posters.

In the apartment above us was a Christian couple. They were friendly and often came down to talk.

"Tom and I are going to a Maranatha concert tonight, Bruce. Why don't you and Lola come with us?"

"I'd like to, Jennie, but we were planning to go to Finigan's tonight."

"How about next Saturday night?"

"I don't know, Jennie, I don't think religion is my thing."

"Bruce, being a Christian is the greatest experience that has ever happened to me."

"Yeah, I know, Jennie, I'm a Christian, too."

"It's different than just being religious," she continued, as if she hadn't heard me. "Jesus wants to come into your life and take control. You just can't believe how neat it is to let Christ control your life. He makes life worth living."

"Yeah? One of my roommates went to one of those concerts and got 'saved.' After that he wouldn't take drugs. You can still be a Christian and use drugs. I think he just went overboard."

Jennie and I talked in circles. She kept asking me to go to church and I kept insisting I didn't need it.

When Lola and I had been living together for three weeks, I realized she was taking between twenty and thirty whites a day. She was becoming a white freak and was on the verge of a nervous breakdown.

"Lola," I suggested, "why don't you go to one of those concerts with Jennie and Tom. It would probably be good for you." She went, and came back with the same look Paul had had.

"I accepted the Lord, Bruce."

"Well, that's nice. But you can still get loaded."

"No, I can't do that anymore."

"Sure, you can." Before she realized what had happened, I had her taking drugs again. I wanted her to get control of herself, not flip out on religion like Paul. I managed to destroy this "Jesus kick."

Lola and I had an agreement. We could date other people, but it was understood we would always be together at the end of the evening.

Our apartment was near Finigan's, and there were many divorced and single chicks living nearby. Most of these girls had kids, but no husbands—and many were quite friendly. I began bouncing from one apartment to the next.

It seemed a dream had come true, but while I was using these girls, they were also using me, and I soon began to feel like a machine.

"Is this all there is to life?" I questioned myself. "There must be more to life than this. This is getting boring."

At Finigan's I met a guy named Kent. "You want to do some business?" I asked.

"Come over to my place and we'll talk about it," he said. "We can get loaded together." Kent was a white freak and was a little edgy. After we were in his apartment, he pulled a revolver on me.

"I want to make sure you're not a narc. Eat this tab of mescaline."

Every drug seller knows narcotics officers never get loaded. Dealers only sell to those who will get loaded in their presence, but this guy was so paranoid he was going to force me at gunpoint.

"Man, it doesn't prove a thing if I eat this. Any narc would take drugs at gunpoint."

Kent left the room for a moment and I took a closer look at the yellow capsule he had given me. It didn't look like any tab of mescaline I'd ever seen. I wondered what was really in it. It could have been poison, for all I knew.

"You're wasting time," Kent accused, coming back into the room. "Take it," he insisted, pushing his gun my way.

"I guess I've no choice." I swallowed the capsule and after fifteen minutes I came on to mescaline.

Kent and I didn't do any business together, but

two weeks later, he came by to tell me of a girl who was selling large quantities of marijuana. She was with the Orange County syndicate and could supply all the grass I wanted.

Kent later introduced me to Cheryl, his contact, a very attractive girl. Cheryl offered me a sample of her grass. I wrote down her address and said I would come over later in the evening.

"After we make the deal, Bruce," she cooed, "we can go out to the movies. We'll have a real good time."

The sample Cheryl gave me was of high quality, and that night I returned to her apartment. She was making a deal with another guy and the buyer was testing its quality. When he was satisfied, he gave her several thousand dollars and carted the grass away. "Far out," I thought, "she can deliver."

"I like the quality of your grass. I'm going to talk to my friends and get some money together. Can you give me a larger sample?"

"Sure, Bruce, I have one kilo left in the apartment. Take this."

"Great. I'll be right back."

I drove over to see several of my friends. They wanted to buy $10,000 worth of grass, but insisted on being present when the deal was made.

"We'll still give you your cut, Bruce, but we don't know these people, and we want to be there when the money changes hands."

They didn't want to do a transaction that night; so I decided to buy the grass with my own money. I picked up all the money I had been able to save since leaving Silverado—a total of $700. Within two weeks

I would double it by selling the weed to my contacts. I drove back to Cheryl's place and gave her the money.

"This is a small amount, Bruce. We never do business with an amount this size, but because I like you, I'll supply the grass."

The guy who had made the earlier deal came back and told Cheryl he had to have more grass.

"Take this kilo," she said. "Bruce just brought it back. It's the only one I have in the place. I'll have more later tonight."

He paid for the kilo and left.

"I'll go get your marijuana," she said.

"Let me go with you," I volunteered.

"I can't let you do that, Bruce. The syndicate is very touchy about who they do business with. Wait here for me; I'll be back in an hour and then we can get things moving." We hugged and kissed a few times before she left. "I have to go now, but we'll do more later."

Cheryl left and I sat down on the couch to wait. An hour went by, but she still had not returned. I walked into the kitchen for a glass of water. Opening the cupboard, I was surprised to find it completely empty. I opened all the other cupboards and the refrigerator. There was not one glass, dish, or piece of food in the place.

I knew I had been ripped off, but my mind did not want to believe it. Cheryl had been too cool. She trusted me with over $200 worth of grass. "She couldn't have ripped me off!"

I rushed into the bedroom, but what I saw only confirmed my fears. The room was bare. "I've been ripped off! What a set-up—and I fell for all of it!'' I sat down on the living room couch and tried to sort it out.

''What can I do to get my money? They'll have to come back for their living room furniture sooner or later. Maybe I should just sit tight.''

After two more hours, the front door swung open and a guy burst in with a gun. He ran around in circles like he was spaced-out.

''Cheryl got busted at the May Co. The narcs moved in on her, and the police were all over the place. There's a quarter of a million dollars' worth of heroin in here and I've got to find it. I'm gonna rip everything open until I find it.''

He pulled out a long knife and started cutting out the cheesecloth underneath the couch. He was probably doing this to scare me, but as he slashed out the bottom of the couch, it was clear he was deadly serious. ''Maybe Cheryl really did get arrested,'' I thought.

''Hey! You didn't squeal on her, did ya?'' he asked suddenly waving his pistol in my face.

''Man, if I did would I be here now?''

''Well, you better get out of here,'' he said, pushing the gun at my nose. ''The police will probably be here any second.''

I didn't like the weapon. This guy was a heroin addict, and there was no telling what he'd pull next. I was ripped off, but there was nothing to do but leave. They would probably clean out their furniture after I left.

I drove over and told Kent what had happened. ''Every cent I had is gone. It took months to get that money together. What a bummer. I've just lost everything again! I could have gotten back into big business with that $700."

"I thought Cheryl was cool. We'll get your money back, Bruce," he said emphatically, while he pulled out his pistol.

"Let's go cruising. We'll find them and I'll kill 'em!"

"Look, I don't want anybody killed. I just want my money back."

"We'll find them. If they ripped you off, man, it's like ripping me off. I was ready to do a deal with them too."

We went up to Cheryl's apartment, and as I had guessed, it was now completely empty. We figured they must live somewhere in the area, so we decided to cruise around until we spotted their cars. Cheryl and her friend drove a custom-fitted silver Jaguar and a new black Cadillac. If we looked long enough we felt we would spot one or both of those cars.

After four hours of driving around the area we were ready to quit when we passed Bob's Restaurant in Costa Mesa. The Cadillac and Jaguar were parked side by side.

"There they are!" I cried excitedly. "Look, there's Cheryl's cars!"

Kent pulled into the lot. As we got out of his car, I began to worry. Had I made a mistake coming after Cheryl? We could get ourselves killed.

When we approached the restaurant door, I could see Cheryl and the heroin addict at a table. "I've got my gun and we're gonna get your money back," Kent announced with determination.

We walked in the front door, past the walk-up counter at which a uniformed policeman was sitting, and marched up to their table. We sat down and calmly looked right in their eyes.

"I . . . er . . . just got out of the hospital," Cheryl fumbled. "I . . . I was busted and he bailed me out, honest." She was obviously startled by our presence.

"I want my money back, all of it!"

Suddenly we heard a click. The heroin addict was wearing a half smile. With a rock-calm voice he announced, "I've got a gun pointed at you two. If you don't get up quietly and walk out of this restaurant, I'll shoot you right here. I don't care if there is a cop over there."

Then he added, "If you pursue this any further, I may not get you tonight, but I'll get you. We have lots of friends, and we'll find you and kill you. Get up right now, or you're both dead."

I looked at Kent. He didn't hesitate. We both stood up, walked past the police officer, and went out the front door.

Once we were in Kent's car he said, "Let's wait for them here. I'll kill them when they come out."

"Man," I replied, "I don't care what you do, I'm splitting. I don't even care about my money any more."

As we pulled away, Kent insisted he was going to come back and get them, but he never did.

Three days later Lola was hired at a massage parlor. She told me about a rich stud who was coming in. He had given her a ride in his brand new Cadillac. I began to wonder if it was the man who had ripped me off.

"Was the car black?"

"Yes. Why?"

"This may be the guy who ripped me off. Get his

license number so I can tell if it's the same guy."
Lola copied down his number, and sure enough, it
turned out to be the same car.

"Man, that's the guy who ripped me off."

"Well, Bruce, he's coming over to spend the night
with me. If you want, I'll signal you when he's asleep
and you can tie him up and take his money."

"No, something will go wrong and I'll get shot. It
was only $700 and it's not worth dying over."

From that point on, I stayed away from Lola.

Chapter Ten
Paint It Black

Nam was released from prison, after serving two
years, and we moved in together. We began to party
almost every night and started dealing together.
Often we went looking for girls just like old times.

One night in Howard's Restaurant in Costa Mesa
we met a girl named Sandy and her friend JoAnn.
They invited us to San Clemente where they were
spending the summer. JoAnn's parents were away
on a two-month vacation, and the girls had the house
to themselves. Bill and I moved in with them.

Sandy became my new girl friend and we began
getting loaded together. She enjoyed the pleasurable
sensations of being high, but had strong guilt
feelings. Sandy was a Christian, and occasionally
she would read her Bible.

"Do you know what it means to be backslidden?"

she asked one day. "It means to be out of fellowship with the Lord. Bruce, you're causing me to backslide."

"I'm a Christian just like you, Sandy. The only difference is I know Jesus doesn't care if we enjoy ourselves by taking drugs."

"I don't know, Bruce. I still feel it's wrong."

"Listen, Sandy, I love you. Do you think I would try to hurt you? I'm only sharing the good things with you."

She couldn't figure me out. I told her I was Christian and she saw that I had Christian bumper stickers on my car, but I didn't act as she thought I should.

One night I overdosed and passed out. The next morning Sandy told me I rose in the middle of the night. "You cursed me with language I never heard before," she said. "Then you blasphemed God and Jesus."

"Really? I did that? I don't remember doing anything after I passed out."

"Bruce, I'm not fooling. You looked so mean last night I thought you were demon-possessed. Your eyes glared at me, and you looked as if you were controlled by the devil."

Sandy's words scared me. I loved God; I didn't hate him. How could I do something like that and not remember it? "Maybe I am demon-possessed," I thought to myself.

My parents called that afternoon to say they were going on their first vacation in five years. They had not left on vacation earlier for fear something bad would happen while they were away.

"Don't worry about a thing," I assured my

98

mother over the phone. "I'll look after the house and make certain nothing happens. I'll even come over and live there while you're away."

I hitchhiked up to Garden Grove to see my parents off. When they had left, I called Nam.

"Hey man, my parents are gone. Bring Sandy and JoAnn and we'll have a party." My parents' spacious backyard was the perfect place for getting loaded. Nam brought the girls up and that night, with forty others, we had a wild time. At the party I became involved with another girl, and Sandy found out. The next night she confronted me.

"Bruce, I want to go back to the Lord. What we're doing is wrong. I don't want to see you any more unless you change. Would you go with me to Calvary Chapel tonight?"

"Church?! We're gonna have another party. I'm not going to take you to church—that's the last thing on my mind tonight."

Sandy looked straight at me. "Bruce, you're sick. You're demon-possessed."

"Oh yeah? You're not the only chick in the world. If you're gonna hassle me, I'll go over to Susie's tonight."

Sandy made me so mad, I was determined to blow her mind. I called Susie up right in front of her and made a date to spend the night at her house. Then I walked out.

That night I got loaded at Susie's. At midnight I phoned my parent's house to check on the party.

"Hi, Bruce," Nam answered. "Things are really happening here! You oughta come back over, man; we're having a blast!"

"You sound wasted, man. Is Sandy still there?"

"Yeah, she's here. She's been preaching at us all night. Just a second." There were noises on the other end of the line, then Sandy picked up the receiver. She started crying and told me how much she loved me. I explained I couldn't come back to the party because I was stoned on reds.

"Don't come back if you're high. It's foggy out, and you'll get killed. Your life is precious, Bruce. God doesn't want you to destroy yourself like that."

Nam came back on the phone and told me Sandy had been talking to everybody at the party about Jesus.

"That's far out, man. I'll see you later."

Early the next morning, I drove back to my parents' house. When I pulled up, there were police cars and ambulances everywhere. The next-door neighbor met me at the curb. "Your girl friend is dead, Bruce."

"You're kidding! I just saw her last night."

I ran into the backyard and was jolted to see Sandy and a friend named Jay lying lifelessly at the edge of the pool. I couldn't believe it; my mind wouldn't accept it.

I suddenly realized the police were searching everywhere for drugs. I panicked because I had hundreds of dollars' worth of drugs hidden in and around the house.

"What's your name?" a plainclothes detective interrupted my thoughts.

"Bruce Danzara."

"You live here?"

"No, this is my parents' house."

The officer asked if I knew the deceased. He was not sure if Sandy and Jay had overdosed and drowned, or if they had been murdered. He told me there would be a homicide investigation.

"Stay in the area, Bruce; we'll want to question you during our investigation."

I was depressed. Sandy had been such a good person. "If only I had stayed home," I blamed myself, "she'd still be alive."

I knew my parents would be heartbroken. The next-door neighbor managed to reach them with the news and they were on their way home.

The next day I was called in for questioning. I played completely innocent. I claimed I hadn't taken drugs for months. The detective seemed to believe me.

That night I could feel eyes watching my parent's place. The police hadn't found the mescaline I had hidden in the backyard. Late that evening I crawled outside to retrieve the evidence, then hid it in an old broken-down car sitting in front of the house.

Sandy's funeral was the next day. Although my father didn't know her well and had never met her parents, he went with me to the funeral.

When we walked into the mortuary chapel I peered into Sandy's casket and my brain was numbed by her pretty face. She looked so alive.

The minister who was handling the funeral preached that Sandy had been led astray. He kept making reference to "the one" who had caused Sandy's life to be cut short. It seemed everyone was looking at me. I was overwhelmed with guilt and the minister's words were ripping into me. I had to work on holding back the tears, but when my father began to cry, I suddenly found myself sobbing out of control.

After the funeral, I talked to the people who had been at the party. Everyone claimed they had passed out by the time Jay and Sandy fell into the pool. Because of my phone call, I knew everyone was awake at midnight, but the police had established 3 A.M. as the time of death. I couldn't know whether my friends were lying.

With the homicide investigation going on, there was the constant fear of being arrested. I wanted to split and go to Oregon where some of my friends had moved.

I had been selling drugs to a fellow named Gordon for a period of six months. Gordon had been talking about making a million-dollar deal. I wanted to make some big deals and retire.

I called Gordon. "This is Bruce. You interested in picking up some mescaline?"

"Yeah, how much you got?"

"Seven hundred dollars' worth."

"Sounds good. Where do you want to meet?"

"The ice cream stand near my house."

"Okay. I'll see you in about thirty minutes."

I went down to the ice cream stand and had a hamburger and coke. After a few minutes Gordon pulled up.

"You got the drugs with you?"

"No, they're at my parents' house."

"Hop in," he said. "Let's get them."

As I got into his car, a strange foreboding sensation grabbed my stomach. I had the distinct feeling we were being followed or watched. "Am I paranoid, or am I just imagining things?" I thought.

We pulled into my parents' driveway. Mom and Dad had gone out to dinner, and I knew we had little time before they returned.

"Wait here. I'll get the drugs."

I casually stepped out of Gordon's car and walked to the wreck in which I had stashed my drugs. I removed the mescaline, quickly climbed back into Gordon's car, and handed him the baggy containing the drugs.

"Just a minute; I have to get the money out of the trunk," Gordon blurted, then jumped from his car.

"Man, this isn't right," I thought. "We're gonna get caught. This is too obvious."

As soon as Gordon had opened the trunk, my door flew open and several hands grabbed my shirt, pulling me out of the car and down to the curb. Four or five cocked guns stabbed at my back and head.

"Freeze, you hippie! This is a bust!"

My mind flashed to my earlier bust and I imagined those guns going off. My body jerked violently out of control and half of my life flashed before my eyes. "Oh, God, help me!" I cried out silently, but God seemed so far away.

They stood me up against the car and shook me down for weapons. "FBI! You're busted!"

Gordon whipped around the car and smiled. "You thought I was your friend, didn't you, Bruce?"

I gave back a half-hearted smile. "Yeah man, you really had me fooled."

They told me I was arrested on eight charges of five to life each and explained my rights. They handcuffed my hands behind my back and pushed me into the rear seat of an unmarked police car. Then they drove off to arrest two friends of mine who had also sold to Gordon.

"Bruce, you don't look like a stupid guy," said one of the agents. "Whatever made you get so messed up?"

"I don't know. I'm really sorry for what I've done." I was trying to sound remorseful so they would let up on me, but in my mind I was thinking, "You pig. What right do you have to interrupt my life like this?"

When we reached my friend's apartment, they told me to slide down on the floor in case there was any gunfire when they arrested Dave and Mary. After a half hour they brought out my friends and drove us all to the Garden Grove police station.

The FBI had been buying drugs from me for six months hoping to make connection with my suppliers. After the drownings, the local police had pushed for my immediate arrest. The three of us were immediately separated and interrogated.

"Where'd you get your drugs, Bruce?"

"I had a lot of sources."

"Where did you get this mescaline?"

"In Laguna Beach. At the taco stand. I just looked for someone who was selling. I bought that mescaline from someone I didn't know."

"What about these drugs?" they asked holding up a plastic bag which contained drugs I had sold to Gordon earlier. "Where did you buy these?"

"The same place, down at that taco stand. Only that time from a different guy."

"That's what everybody claims. Nobody ever knows who they got their drugs from. You're just copping out."

"It's the truth, man."

"If you cooperate with us, things will go easier on you, Bruce. See this piece of paper?"

The officer was holding a letter which had my name on it, the charges against me, and all the drugs they had found. It was addressed to the President of the United States.

"The President is very interested in knowing what's happening with pushers. They're gonna hang every pusher they get. They won't be lenient any more. They're gonna send you to prison. If you cooperate you'll get off easier."

"Man, there's nothing else I can tell you. I don't know who I got the drugs from. I'm cooperating in every way I know how. I can't tell you what I don't know."

"Do you know anyone in the brotherhood?" another officer asked.

"No, I don't know anyone in that organization," I lied.

"Are you in the brotherhood?"

"No way, man."

"How did you ever get mixed up in all this? You don't look like a dumb guy."

"I don't know. I really don't know. It just happened, I guess. I was getting sick of the whole thing and planning to take the seven hundred from Gordon and travel up to Oregon. I have a friend in Grants Pass and was going up to see him."

The agents looked at each other. "Grants Pass! That's where the brotherhood have one of their headquarters. You just wanted to get away from everything, didn't you?"

"Wow! I didn't know that was the headquarters for the brotherhood. Honest."

"You're really in the brotherhood, aren't you?"

"No way, man. Look, I told you I'm not in that organization. My friend in Oregon had no connection with them either."

After a long interrogation the officers seemed convinced I was telling the truth—for the most part. Apparently they had arrested a number of my friends who were in the brotherhood and wanted to make sure I wasn't a member. All those connected with the organization were given high bails to keep them in jail, some as high as a million dollars.

Dave, Mary, and I were taken to the Orange County Jail where we spent the night. Next day we were taken to the Federal Courthouse in Los Angeles. In the holding cell we discovered we were rubbing shoulders with bank robbers, hijackers, and counterfeiters.

We were arraigned that day and my bail was set at $50,000. My parents put their house up to meet my bail and within four hours I was able to go home.

The shock of the drownings had still not worn off, and I could tell this new development was depressing my parents even further. I couldn't believe it myself. Everything was turning black.

All my friends told me to leave the country. "You're gonna be in jail the rest of your life. You might just as well split," they counseled. I seriously considered leaving the country, but I knew if I did my parents would lose their house.

After a week out on bail, I picked up the evening paper and saw a front page headline which read, "GRAND JURY DRUG INDICTMENTS RELEASED." The article said that eighteen people were being indicted for the sale of dangerous drugs. Only five had been arrested so far.

I looked down at the article to see if any of my friends were on the list and discovered Nam's name. Right below his name, I discovered my own! The news article claimed there were four counts of five years to life against me and that bail was already set at $25,000.

"I don't even remember who I sold to. Maybe they've made a mistake."

I knew they could be coming for me at any moment. I had to get out of the house. I ran out the door and went to a friend's house. I called my public defender.

"The best thing for you to do, Mr. Danzara, is to turn yourself in. If you turn yourself in, they'll be a lot easier on you. But it's your decision."

"This is really a drag. Things are really getting bad. I don't know what to do."

I spent the night at my friend's and called home the next morning to tell my parents what had happened. My father answered the phone.

"Bruce, five narcotics officers came looking for you last night. When I opened the front door they shoved guns in my face and almost shot me. Bruce, I'm worried for you. Those men are trigger happy. You better turn yourself in so you don't get shot. If they think you're trying to escape, they'll kill you."

"Okay, Dad, I'll turn myself in."

My father picked me up and we went to the sheriff's office. They searched for an hour before they found the correct indictment and booked me in. It was Friday and I knew they would do nothing with me until Monday morning.

They assigned me to a large open jail cell called a dorm. There were approximately forty prisoners in the cell. As I walked in that Friday afternoon, three prisoners whistled and made jokes about my long hair. They were rather hard-looking types with shaved heads. They challenged me to fight, but I ignored them and found an empty bunk at the other end of the cell.

My bunkmate turned out to be a friend from Silverado days. Because Brent was in the brotherhood the judge had set his bail at $250,000. He had already been in jail six months and was still waiting for his trial.

"Hey, Brent, what's with those three guys with the shaved heads? What's their trip?"

"Those guys are animals. They're insane. Everybody in here is afraid of them. They were busted for armed robbery and are on their way to prison. They feel they've nothing to lose."

When we came back from dinner that night, the three thugs began to whistle at another prisoner with long hair. They kept it up for three hours, until the lights went out. Then they jumped him on his bunk. They kicked and hit him mercilessly, then pulled him screaming into the showers. Stripping off his clothes, they kicked his body to a bloody pulp.

Not a soul moved to help him. His cries for help made everyone shudder, but the fear of being next kept all of us in our own bunks.

Finally the three men turned the shower on their prey and came back into the dorm. They were laughing at their victim's whimpering and were obviously very proud of themselves.

"Man, this is insane. We can all stop those guys," I complained to Brent.

"Yeah, but everybody's afraid it will happen to them next."

The next day at breakfast, it was obvious the prisoner with long blond hair had been beaten badly.

His face was puffed up and he was in a daze. I marveled he didn't go to the guards, but they had threatened to kill him if he did, and he was too scared to try for help.

Saturday night they jumped him again and began beating the poor man in his bunk.

"Oh, Jesus, help me," he cried. He was talking to Christ like he was in the room. His cries ripped into me, but fear for my own safety was too great.

When the tormentors had completed their attack and had returned to their bunks, one of them yelled back at his quivering body, "Shut up about that Jesus stuff or we'll let you have it again, you fag!"

"Hey," one of the others chimed in, "let's sing about Jesus."

They began to sing all kinds of Protestant hymns, the kind of songs they sing in jail chapels, only these three depraved individuals began to insert foul words and make each song blasphemous.

The songs were not familiar to me, but each time they blasphemed God something cut deeply into my heart. I couldn't stand their words. I was getting sick to my stomach listening to them sing.

"Oh, God," I prayed, "I want out of here so badly." But in my heart I felt destined to be in jail for the next fifteen or twenty years. Brent had convinced me I would never get out again. There were just too many charges against me.

At breakfast on Sunday, Brent and I decided to inform the guards what was happening. We hesitated, and at the last second decided not to tell. The risk was too great.

That night, they set their victim's blanket on fire. He woke up screaming. He burned himself and singed his hair trying to put out the flames. By now he was in shock. He was incoherent and stuttered when he tried to talk.

Monday morning on the way to chow they jumped him again. They hit and kicked him a few times, then began to apologize as if they were truly sorry for what they had done.

After breakfast, Brent and I made certain we were the last ones to leave the mess hall. We had not said a word to each other that morning, but we both knew what we had to do. We told a guard what was happening and quickly joined the other prisoners so no one would know who told.

On Monday I was arraigned in court, and to my amazement, was released on my own recognizance because I had turned myself in. It was an unbelievable relief to be free again.

Chapter Eleven
The End of My Rainbow

My life had turned black. Sandy's death had been the beginning, but two major arrests had brought my world crashing down, and I now had a total of twelve counts of five-years-to-life hanging over my head. In addition to these federal and state charges, I had been arrested on two other occasions for possession of drugs, and these trials were also pending. If all this wasn't enough, Santa Barbara County was trying to get me to go to court over a trespassing violation which I had failed to pay.

Life looked bleak. Twenty-three years old and I would probably spend the rest of my life in prison. Now even my friends avoided me because of my depressive attitude.

One night I had an urge to go to Howard's Restaurant in Costa Mesa. I got a ride to the restaurant, then by myself I sat down to drink coffee and get my mind together. Howard's always had lots of activity, and it helped me to be alone in a crowd.

At midnight, a friend named Gary walked in. He bounced over to my booth and sat down.

"What's happening, Bruce?"

"Not much. How about you?"

Gary had a large, almost disgusting smile on his face, and for the first time I could remember, he looked me right in the eyes. "Man, the Lord just sent me here to you. You've got a need. You're in trouble, and you need the Lord."

I started laughing. Gary was really funny. "What kind of trip are you on? Don't tell me you're one of those Jesus freaks?"

"Yeah, man, I'm a Christian. I accepted the Lord three days ago."

Gary did look happy, but I was in no mood to be preached at. "Man, I'm a Christian too. Why are you trying to freak me out?"

"Bruce, I was home sleeping an hour ago. I woke up, and the Lord told me to come down here because there was a need. I didn't know what the need was until I walked into the restaurant and saw you."

I asked Gary if he knew about my arrests.

"Wow, man. I didn't know you got busted. See, you need the Lord. You've *really* got a need."

"Ah, everybody needs the Lord," I responded sarcastically. "We all need God."

111

"Bruce, come with me to Calvary Chapel. Tomorrow night it's gonna be really good, and it will help you."

A lot of my friends had gone to that church and gotten "saved." I wanted no part of that trip.

"I don't want anyone preaching at me. I've got enough problems without that."

"No one will preach to you. Everything will be cool. You'll really enjoy it."

"I don't know, man."

"Look, Bruce, in the situation you're in, you need to play it cool. Besides, God may help you with your problems."

I had to admit there was everything to gain and nothing to lose. It would take a miracle to get me out of trouble, and I needed all the help I could get. "Okay, I'll go with you. But just this once."

I'd heard about Calvary Chapel on and off for four years. Sandy had attended there before she met me. If I went to that church, there would be a confrontation.

Now, for some reason, I found myself drawn to the place. In the back of my mind I hoped something good would happen there, but I'd had religion all my life, and it had never satisfied.

The next night Gary met me and together we hitchhiked down to Costa Mesa. I had no idea what to expect, but was surprised by what I saw. The church was surrounded by fields, and it wasn't a church at all. It was a king-sized circus tent. I stopped walking when I realized where we were going.

"No way, man. You're not getting me into any

revival, holy roller circus. No way! I was warned as a child about places like this!"

"Look, Bruce. Nobody's gonna do anything weird. They don't run around and scream, honest."

"I don't know about this."

"Look," Gary assured, "if anything weird happens, we'll get up and leave. Okay?"

"Well, all right."

We continued toward the tent, and the sensation that I was attending my own funeral came over me. With each step we took, something in my brain cried, "This is the end of Bruce."

Once inside the tent, I was overwhelmed by the warmth of the crowd. Never had I seen so many people with happy expressions of love and concern on their faces. It wasn't just the look on their faces, there was an unusual atmosphere in the tent. I could sense a spirit of harmony and acceptance of outsiders. These people seemed to have something special they wanted to share with the world. On acid I had often felt vibrations of love coming from those around me. But this was more powerful than anything I had experienced. The vibrations were much stronger.

"Wow," I said to Gary. "These people aren't loaded."

"They're high on God, Bruce."

"Wow!" was all I could say. Everyone I knew got loaded on drugs. I couldn't comprehend how so many people could look so happy and not be on drugs.

In the crowd were young people with long hair and beards sitting next to older people with suits and ties.

Yet there seemed to be no generation gap.

Gary and I had arrived late, and the minister was already speaking. The preacher was the same man who had spoken at Sandy's funeral. Gary told me he was Chuck Smith, the pastor of the church.

He was sharing Bible verses which Sandy had read to me. Most of what he said was familiar because many Christians had said the very same things to me. But somehow his words about Christ made better sense than ever before. Something deep inside cried, "You need Christ. He's the answer to your problems."

I really wanted to know God. It was obvious I didn't know him the way this minister and the people in the tent knew him.

"Jesus wants to come into your life," the preacher continued. "He wants to give you an abundant life. In Revelation 3:20, he says: 'Behold, I stand at the door and knock. If any man hears my voice and opens the door, I will come in to him and sup with him and he with me.' Jesus wants to come into your heart and have fellowship with you right now."

For the first time in my life I realized Christ wanted to come into my life. God had always been somewhere up in outer space. I had never heard he wanted to come into my heart.

"But what do Christians do?" I thought. "They don't get loaded or have sex. If I become a Christian it's really gonna be boring. On the other hand, jail is gonna be pretty boring anyway; maybe I don't have much to lose."

The minister continued by quoting another verse. " 'If any man be in Christ, he is a new creature. Old things are passed away, behold all things become new.' Christ is offering you a new life."

114

I knew the only thing that could possibly help me was a fresh start. That Bible verse seemed to promise the only thing that could make a difference in my life: a new heart.

I desperately wanted a new life. I wanted everything that the minister was talking about, but as he continued, my mind argued with my emotions. "This is just religion. You've already gone through this once. This is nothing. But if there is something to this," I reasoned, "I should give it a chance. I want this to be real."

I didn't need another trip into religion. My brain couldn't take the disappointment if I only psyched myself into believing something. I had to know the truth. Was Jesus really able to do what the preacher claimed?

"God," I prayed silently, "if you're real, help me. I'm sorry for what I've done. I'm miserable inside. Come into my life and take over. I don't care about jail. I'll go to prison for the rest of my life if you'll just show yourself to me. I'll give up sex, drugs— everything, if you'll just be real to me."

The second I uttered that prayer, something happened! The fog lifted. My confusion was gone. The oppressive guilt from Sandy's drowning disappeared. An overwhelming sense of peace filled me up. There was no fear of the future; no more fear of jail.

I had firmly believed in love, but I was experiencing a new kind of love. It was being dumped on me. For the first time in my life I felt an unselfish desire to meet other people's needs. It was a love that did not demand personal gratification.

I had often wondered what Christians meant when they talked about being "born again." Now I knew.

No one had to tell me I was born again. I felt like a kid. Life had become fresh and alive. I had come into the world all over again.

The service was over, and the minister asked those who wanted to become Christians to come forward and talk to some counselors. I didn't go forward because I was already a Christian. Gary gave me a big hug.

"You got saved, didn't you, Bruce?"

"Man," I said through a wide smile, "I'm born again, and I know it."

Across the aisle I saw a familiar face. It was a friend from my school days.

"Hey, are you a Christian, too?" I asked.

"Yeah," he answered, "I got saved over a year ago."

"I don't know what to say. I'm just so — — — happy!"   Before I could catch myself, I had used a swear word. My friend looked at me strangely.

"Oh, I'm sorry," I said. "That was a terrible thing to say."

For seven years that swear word and many others had been part of my vocabulary, but I knew they were no longer for me.

"Bruce met Jesus tonight," Gary explained to my friend. He smiled and hugged me.

"Praise the Lord, Bruce. You're a brother now."

Gary and I walked out of the tent, and it suddenly dawned on me I had no desire for drugs or alcohol. All through the service my body had been aching for some kind of intoxicant. Now my system felt completely relieved. I hadn't felt like this in years.

"Gary, I'm not going through withdrawal anymore. I have no desire for drugs. It's a miracle."

Gary and I decided to hitchhike to Howard's Restaurant where we had been the night before. On the way down, we had fellowship in the Lord—a new experience for me. Because I didn't know any Christian songs, Gary taught me one song after another, and we sang and praised the Lord all the way to the restaurant.

I was overwhelmed by what had happened to me. I didn't know what the future held, but I no longer had the desire to please myself. I wanted to serve God.

"Bruce," Gary warned, "the devil is gonna tempt you. He's gonna throw the old life at you."

"Don't worry, man, it's cool. I'm ready."

I had always defended free use of drugs and sex as being important pleasures in life. Somehow I knew that those pleasures would no longer be a part of my life. I had a new sense of balance—a new sense of right and wrong.

When we arrived at the restaurant, it was crowded, so we put our names on the list for a booth. While we waited, I noticed a girl whom I had been trying to make it with for a long time. Since my arrests she hadn't given me the time of day. For some reason, possibly because of the big smile on my face, she walked up and gave me a warm hug.

"What are you smiling about, Bruce?" she asked coyly.

"I just got saved at Calvary Chapel. I just became a Christian."

"Are you putting me on? How'd you like to come home with me tonight?

She was extremely attractive, and normally I wouldn't have hesitated, but I knew what I had to say.

"No, I don't do that anymore."

"Oh, come on, Bruce," she said, pushing up against me. "I know you like me. Why don't you come over to my place and spend the night with me?"

"I'm sorry, but now that I'm a Christian, I don't do that anymore." I could tell she was getting uptight, so I tried to explain. "You're a neat chick, but I don't make love with anyone now."

"You've flipped out! You can't handle prison, and you're using religion as a crutch." She stomped off to join her friends.

Gary smiled at me. "What did I tell you? Satan's already trying to drag you back to the old life."

Our names were called and we walked to a booth. But once we sat down, another chick I had been trying to seduce came up to our table. She made the same offer the first girl had made.

My mind immediately flashed to Jesus, and I prayed silently for the strength to say no a second time. It was as if Satan was saying, "Bruce, you're so popular; all these girls want you. Why not take her up on it?" I realized Satan was motivating these girls, and I had to say no. When I told her where I stood, she too, stomped off.

Before an hour went by, still another girl came up and made a similar proposition. I couldn't believe all the attention the devil was giving me. I rejected her offer and felt an overwhelming power, a spiritual power which gave me the strength to be good. It was a power which I had never before possessed.

By now most of my friends in the coffee shop knew I was a Christian. But even though Gary and I were reading his Bible, people kept coming up to ask me for drugs.

"Got any reds, man?" one guy asked.

"Sure," I replied, handing him a small red tract with Bible verses in it that Gary had with him.

When he realized what I had given him, he threw it back at me and said, "Hey man, what's your trip?"

"I just got saved."

"Far out, man. You just freaked out and turned to religion. You can *have* your religion."

Gary and I stayed at the restaurant, drinking coffee, until six o'clock in the morning. He suggested I stay at the Christian house where he was living. We hitchhiked down Pacific Coast Highway until we came to Corona Del Mar. Gary was staying at a place called the Margarette House.

The house was run by Rick Nabors and had four guys living in it. I met Rick and shared some of my past and how I had gotten saved. He told me I was welcome at the house.

By now Gary and I were exhausted. Someone turned on a tape by a group called "Love Song," and we fell asleep listening to beautiful Christian music.

When I awoke that afternoon, I called my parents.

"Mom, guess what? I just gave up drugs. I've become a Christian."

My parents were excited that I had given up drugs, but they didn't grasp what had happened to me. They couldn't understand how this Christian experience could be any different from the religious training I had received as a child.

That afternoon, Gary and I hitchhiked over to the apartment of Graham and Sylvia, two of my close friends. We had gotten loaded together just a few days earlier. Sylvia opened the door and invited us in.

"Graham's in Texas. What are you doing with a Bible, Bruce?"

"I got saved last night. I accepted the Lord."

"Have you freaked out? What do you mean, you accepted the Lord?"

"I asked Jesus to come into my life, and I don't take drugs anymore."

I began to tell Sylvia what had happened the night before. She could see by the radical change in my life that God had really done something. She kept agreeing with me, as if she couldn't get enough of what I was saying.

Occasionally Sylvia asked a question. Somehow, I was able to find answers from the Bible for each question. It was as though God was actually speaking through me—a powerful and unusual experience.

"We're on our way to church. You want to come with us?"

"No, I don't think so."

"Well, we'll see you later then. The Lord bless you."

We were out the door when Sylvia changed her mind. "Just a second, just a second. I want to go."

She grabbed a Bible someone had given her and came running out of the apartment. The three of us attended one of Calvary Chapel's evening Bible studies. Sylvia was touched by the service, but she did not make any decision.

The Margarette House possessed a warm atmosphere. There were pictures of Christ on most of the walls along with verses from the Bible. Christian

120

music was almost always playing in the background.

All the people living in the house were strangers to me, yet they instantly became my best friends. They were willing to share whatever they could to help me. I could see their love was sincere and motivated by Christ. I understood what the Bible meant when it said Christians became one in Christ.

Rick Nabors, the elder of the house, was the son of a wealthy car dealer. He had given up much to serve the Lord. He knew the Bible well and led studies often. He gave me my own Bible, a King James Version.

I had read parts of the Bible as a non-Christian, but now it opened up before my eyes. It made sense for the first time. It was like the book was alive. Every word meant something to me. Each passage had heavy implications for my personal life.

I read verses like First Thessalonians 5:17, which said, "Pray without ceasing." I learned I should have a prayerful attitude at all times and bring every problem to God.

Verse eighteen read, "In everything give thanks, for this is the will of God in Christ Jesus concerning you." In good and bad situations I was to thank God; both in little things and big things I was to praise the Lord. Everything that happened during the day was for a reason, and I was to thank God for it.

The meaning of the Bible opened up because I had met the author of the Book. My hunger for the pages of the Bible was unbelievable. I couldn't get enough of it. I spent hours reading it each day—every second not taken up doing something else.

Christ said the Holy Spirit would be our teacher; I prayed that God's Spirit would teach me everything I needed to know. All my questions about God were answered in full. There were no doubts now about what I had done. I knew Christ was God, and I had to live for him.

Rick led Bible studies daily at the Margarette House. We had prayer meetings almost every night, and my fellowship with the guys in the house was rich. I had more friends than ever before.

As a non-Christian, I had always considered myself a loving person; but I began to realize my love had been selfish. I had wanted to possess things. With Christ in my heart, my attitude was different. I realized that real love was giving, expecting nothing in return. It was a new experience.

Although the Lord had already taken away the overwhelming guilt from my former way of life, it was encouraging to hear the results of the police investigation on Sandy's death. There was no evidence that she had been high on drugs the night she died. Apparently Jay had fallen into the pool and was too loaded to help himself. Sandy must have been the only sober person at the party, and probably jumped in to save him. In his attempts to save himself, Jay caught her in a "death hold" and they went down together.

In many ways my whole life-style had been responsible for Sandy's death. But God gave me the calm assurance that she too had forgiven me. I knew that someday I would see her again in heaven.

During the first week after my conversion, Gary and I kept going to Howard's Restaurant. By now all my friends had heard of my conversion. Most thought I had gone off the deep end, but some were quietly watching me because they couldn't comprehend how a guy facing so much prison could be happy. They wanted to see if it would wear off. We led several of my friends to Christ at the restaurant.

Gary and I also went back to see Sylvia. Graham had returned from Texas, so we witnessed to both of them. While we were sharing, Graham lit up a joint.

"Are you sure this doesn't bother you?" he asked.

"If that's your thing, go ahead and do it. But you can have more happiness in Christ. He'll change your whole life, and you won't need drugs. I don't need them anymore."

We talked at length about Christ and his power to transform, but didn't seem to be making too much headway.

"You know," I said finally, "if you guys really love each other, you'd get married."

"Well, that's just a piece of paper," Graham objected.

"If you love each other, how would that paper make a difference? It just declares you do love each other and makes it hard to cop out on one another later. If you really do love each other, you wouldn't be scared by a piece of paper."

Graham and Sylvia looked at each other and I could tell the Lord was dealing with their hearts. "We want to talk for a bit," Graham said, and they disappeared into the bedroom. In five minutes they came back into the living room.

"We want to accept the Lord," Graham blurted out. "We want to become Christians and get married, too."

"Praise the Lord!" Gary and I responded together.

"But there's one problem," Graham went on. "I

still have a kilo of marijuana. All our money is tied up in that kilo and we could never get married without it.''

''Well, you've got to get rid of it.''

The four of us went out to eat, and I could tell the marijuana was going to be a real problem. We decided to pray for God to take care of the situation.

''Lord, you take care of this problem. You know Graham and Sylvia want to give their lives to you. So bring about the circumstances and conditions so they can totally give their lives to you.''

After dinner we went back to their apartment and discovered someone had broken in and stolen all their money and the kilo of marijuana! Now nothing stood between them and Christ.

Sylvia and Graham made public decisions at Calvary to accept Christ. They made an appointment with the pastor and set a wedding date, two weeks away. We all praised the Lord together.

Chapter Twelve
Wonder of Wonders

At one of the evening Bible studies at Calvary, Pastor Chuck Smith announced there would be a mass baptism at Corona Del Mar beach. I began to think about being baptized. I wanted to follow the Lord's command.

I went down to the beach that Friday with Gary and Rick and some other Christian friends. I had never seen so many Christians before. There were several thousand on the beach and at least a thousand people at the water's edge waiting to be baptized.

"Are all these people new Christians?" I asked Rick. "They didn't all come to know the Lord recently, did they?"

"They're new Christians all right. Most of them came to the Lord at Calvary."

"That's heavy. Hey, I'd like to have my parents see my baptism."

I ran off the beach and traveled the few short blocks to the Margarette House and called my parents. They said they would come down right away.

I walked back down to the beach and waited at the water's edge. By the time it was dark, my parents had still not arrived and almost everyone had been baptized. When my turn finally came, I told Chuck Smith my parents had not arrived. We waited a few more minutes, but when they still did not appear, I told him to go ahead.

Chuck led me out until we were waist deep in the ocean. He talked to me for a few minutes. "Since you have professed your faith in Jesus Christ, I now baptize you in the name of the Father, the Son, and the Holy Spirit."

With that statement, he dunked me below the surface, then quickly raised me up again. He concluded by saying, "Amen," when I was back on my feet.

Chuck gave me a big hug, then the two of us walked up onto the beach. As we reached the large campfires burning on the sand, my parents walked up. They had missed my baptism, but I was still happy. I could tell they were happy for me.

My parents had never seen so many Christians.

Around each campfire were forty or fifty Christians all singing praises to God. I could tell they were moved by what they saw.

"Mom and Dad, why don't you come see where I'm staying?"

We walked off the beach and traveled the few short blocks to the Margarette House. Several of my friends were already present and everyone was high on the Lord.

"Hey, brothers, I want you to meet my folks. Mom and Dad, this is Rick, Lonnie, Woody, and Jim." I also introduced eleven others present that night.

As we sat around talking about how all our lives had been changed, I noticed my father was becoming emotional. "It's hard to believe how you've changed, Bruce. It would be so nice if Dan could change, too. But I guess it's asking too much for him to come off drugs too."

Dan was my brother, and he was on heroin. Dad was quite concerned about him.

"He can be changed, Dad. I know he can. If God can transform my heart, there's no reason he can't do it to Dan's heart too."

"Why don't we pray for him?" one of the brothers suggested.

"Oh, that would be nice," Dad replied, but I could tell by the expression in his voice that he thought the situation hopeless.

We bowed our heads, and one by one each Christian prayed. I couldn't believe their discernment. They didn't know Dan, yet they prayed beyond their knowledge. The presence of God was in the room in a powerful way, and everyone else sensed it too.

126

After we had prayed, one of the brothers addressed my dad. "The Lord spoke to me while we prayed. Dan is going to quit drugs."

Both my parents were sobbing uncontrollably. "Thank you so much for your prayers and your love. We . . . don't know what to say."

Mom and Dad went home, but I was still floating. I wanted them to become Christians in the worst way. I began to pray for their salvation daily.

Next week my dad informed me that Dan had stopped taking drugs! He had finally reached the end of his rope. My father knew the moment he heard of Dan's decision that our prayers had been answered. Dad's attitude toward my encounter with Christ was beginning to become very positive.

After living apart for two weeks, Graham and Sylvia were married at Calvary. I attended the service in the chapel, then went to the tent to see the Saturday night concert.

As I stood at the back of the crowded tent, a strange feeling flooded over me. It was an unearthly sensation, as if Satan was on the prowl, and I broke into a cold sweat.

Suddenly sharp pains ripped into my back. In front of my eyes two explosions went off in the midst of the crowd, and I imagined people flying in every direction. It was like an acid flashback, but I had not had any since my conversion. I knew somewhere something was wrong.

"Lord," I prayed, "I don't know what's happening, but bind the power of Satan." Instantly the pain in my back disappeared. The sight in front of my eyes dissolved and the oppressive spirit that I had sensed vanished.

The next day I was talking to Mike MacIntosh and Don McClure, two of Calvary's ministers, and they told me of a strange occurrence at the tent the night before. A disturbed marine appeared in the tent aisle (on the other side of the tent from where I had been standing) and started threatening if he didn't get a seat he would blow the place up. He had grenades in both hands! Pastors Romaine and McClure quickly subdued him. They called the police and soon discovered the soldier was AWOL. In the trunk of his car were enough explosives to level a city block!

"Wow," I thought to myself, "that's what I saw the night before. It must have been a vision."

Because there were a few weeks before my trial on state charges, Gary and I decided to go north on an evangelistic trip. Neither of us had a car or money, so we decided to hitchhike up the coast. Before we left, we went to Calvary Chapel and talked to Pastor Chuck.

"We're going up north and don't have any money. Is there any way we can get some tracts?"

Chuck reached into his pocket and pulled out some money. "Take this and go buy some tracts."

Gary and I were touched by Chuck's generosity. Calvary had many tracts, and he could easily have provided some of them. Instead, he gave us money out of his own pocket.

Gary and I bought a large supply of Christian literature. We had a road-bag which we filled with Christian tracts, New Testaments, and every other piece of literature we could get our hands on.

For so much of my life I needed drugs to bring life into focus. The wonders of nature were not exciting unless I was high. I had used marijuana and LSD to fill the void in my life. But it was useless; the more I took, the emptier I became. As a Christian I was happily sober for the first time in seven years. God had filled me to overflowing and I wanted to share my experience with the world. I didn't need drugs anymore—I had Christ!

As we traveled up the coast, we were exposed to people on drugs. Once we climbed into a van filled with marijuana smoke.

"Want some grass, man?"

"No, thanks," I said, "we've got Jesus."

It wasn't that I was repulsed by the smell of marijuana. It still smelled just as sweet, but I didn't need it now.

"Why not, man? You can be into Jesus and still get high."

"No way. If I smoke your grass, I'll come down. I'm so high on Jesus, drugs can only bring me down."

I was beginning to understand that Scripture where Jesus says you shall know the truth and the truth will set you free. I never had great willpower, but Christ gave me the power to be free from my own wrong desires.

As we hitchhiked up the coast, every ride gave us opportunities to share our relationship with Christ. Three or four people who picked us up became Christians. We were taken to dinner and often given a place to sleep by the people we led to the Lord.

In Santa Cruz, Gary met his girl friend and the three of us went to Sambo's for dinner. While we waited for our food, Gary and I pulled out our Bibles and began to read.

I looked up to see a man rush into the restaurant.

He had a strange look in his eyes, and the moment he stepped into the building he glared right at me. He stared for a long moment, glanced nervously around the restaurant, then came up to our table.

"Can I sit here?"

His eyes were dilating back and forth and my first guess was he had overdosed on LSD. He looked crazy.

"Sure," I said, realizing there were many other booths at which he could sit. When he sat down, he looked at my Bible, then across at Gary's.

"I'm the devil," he announced dramatically. "I was on the cross next to Christ."

A cold shiver ran up my back. I had this weird feeling he was who he claimed to be.

"You're not the devil," I smiled. "Jesus loves you; don't you know that?"

When I said Jesus' name, the man's face flinched and he seemed to break out in goose bumps. Our food was brought to the table and our strange guest began to mumble to himself as if he were speaking another language.

"I'm gonna kill the President," he continued once the waitress had gone. "I'm gonna rape every virgin in this country. I've already killed a couple of people and there isn't anything I won't do."

Gary's girl friend was trying to sink into the leather booth. Our satanic guest was foul-mouthed, and in every sentence he blasphemed God. But when he cursed the blood of Jesus, he had gone too far.

"You're demon-possessed!" I accused him. "Greater is he that is in me than he that is in you."

"Oh yeah!" he cried, pulling out a big

130

straightedged razor. "You wanna go outside and find out who's greatest?"

"No way, man."

"Wait!" he cried, jumping up. The waitresses all turned to watch him as he disappeared into the rest room.

"Get him out of here," Gary's girl friend begged. "I can't handle any more of this."

Suddenly he came running out of the head yelling, "There's a bomb! Someone put a bomb in the head! Everybody get out!"

People jumped up and ran outside. The cooks ducked down behind the counter. One of the waitresses picked up the phone to call the police. A spirit of fear descended on the restaurant.

"There's no bomb in here," Gary cautioned. "This guy's just trying to cause fear."

Immediately the Scripture which says "Satan goes around like a roaring lion" came to my mind. I knew this guy had to be demon-possessed.

"Come on, you guys!" he yelled at us. "We'd better get out of here before we get blown up! Let's go over to my house!"

"Nope. We're not leaving," Gary said in a matter-of-fact tone.

"You're gonna get blown up!" he yelled.

"Look, man, you're demon-possessed," I announced again. "Right now, in the name of Jesus Christ, I command the spirit to come out of you."

I didn't know what I was doing. The ministers at Calvary had counseled Christians to avoid dealing with the demon-possessed unless you knew what you were doing. But I had no choice.

We started praying for him out loud. The more we prayed, the more he cursed God. He began to run up and down the restaurant aisle yelling and swearing. The police finally walked through the front door and grabbed him.

"What's wrong with this guy?" one of the officers asked.

"He's sick," Gary responded. "He needs help."

The rest of the evening we sat and talked about that poor demoniac.

The next day, we left Gary's girl friend and continued hitchhiking up the coast. While we were traveling, we heard of a Christian commune called the Lighthouse, near Cresent City.

The commune was on the coast next to an old lighthouse. It was a large place with a number of buildings. The Christians owned a good deal of the nearby town. One of the girls living at the commune had known Gary two years earlier in Southern California when they had both been non-Christians. We rejoiced at this chance meeting of two friends, now related in Christ.

"Let's go up to Oregon," I suggested. "I haven't been to Oregon since I was a little kid. I'll probably be in jail for the rest of my life and I'd sure like to see some beautiful wilderness before I go to court."

We caught more rides and traveled up to Wonder, Oregon. I was looking for Dale (the brother of the guy who turned me on to grass), a friend from non-Christian days. I had lost his address but Wonder was so small we found him.

Dale was living in a house in the midst of a beautiful meadow. Altogether there were twenty people from Orange County living in Wonder. They sold crafts to the tourists and lived simply.

We stayed with Dale for four days. He was into yoga and transcendental meditation and had several swamis he looked up to. When we shared our faith he was quite unresponsive.

"The Bible says 'there is only one mediator between God and Man.' Jesus is the only way you can get to God the Father."

· "Well, that's just what *you* say," Dale responded negatively.

"It's not important what I say or think, Dale. It's what God says in his Word."

Two miles down the road toward Grants Pass was a girl named Kathy with whom Dale spent much time. She lived in a small house in the middle of the forest with her daughter.

We spent a whole night talking to Kathy about the Lord. She asked many questions and seemed moved by God's power when we showed her verses from the Bible. Kathy didn't make a decision, but for the rest of our stay in Wonder, she spent lots of time listening to us.

We left Oregon and hitchhiked back down the coast. Near Crescent City we stepped out of a car in the middle of nowhere. While we waited for another ride, Gary and I began to sing Christian songs.

An old Chevy drove by, packed with seven guys. As it passed, the occupants swore at us and shook their fists. One guy stuck his head out the window and yelled something about our being girls. Both Gary and I still had long hair; mine reached down to my waist.

As their car came to a stop down the road, Gary looked at me. I knew what he was thinking. We were a long way from civilization and we could easily be wiped out.

"Man, we've had it. They can kill us and push our bodies into the ocean, and nobody will ever know. We better start praying."

We dropped our heads. "Lord, we ask you in Jesus' name to protect us from physical harm. Bind the power of Satan."

They turned their car and headed in our direction. Another car appeared from nowhere, and even though we didn't have our thumbs out, it stopped in front of us.

"You need a ride?" the driver said.

"Yeah! Let us in quick," we answered. "That car is coming after us."

"That car there?" he asked.

"Yeah!"

"Get in; let's get out of here!" he said, and accelerated before I could shut the car door.

"You came just in time. Those guys were gonna beat us up and we just prayed for a ride."

"Are you Christians?"

"We sure are."

"Well, praise the Lord!" he smiled. "So am I."

For a couple hundred miles the three of us praised God and sang Christian songs. We had a good time of fellowship. That night we ate dinner at our ride's house above San Francisco. The next day we proceeded down the coast and made it to Costa Mesa.

After our arrival in Orange County, Gary and I were hitchhiking across town, when on the spur of the moment, we decided to take a short-cut through a residential area. As we were walking, I heard my name being called. Then I heard Gary's name. We turned to see Kathy, the girl we had witnessed to four days earlier in Oregon, standing at the other end of the street. She had a big smile on her face.

"What are you doing here?" we asked. "We left you in Oregon."

"I accepted the Lord! I'm a Christian! Come in, I live at the Lord's House."

Gary and I looked at each other with expressions of wonder, then floated behind her into the house. It was unbelievable that Kathy could be in huge Orange County only four days later, and that we should run into her.

Kathy related how she had cried the night we left Wonder. We were the first two men she had ever met who were not after her body. She knew we were interested in what was best for her, and that realization broke her down. She knew we had something she needed.

"Not knowing where to turn, I pulled out these tracts you left me and started reading them. As I read them, God spoke to me. I followed the instructions in the booklet and asked God into my heart.

"I knew immediately I was a Christian. I also knew I had to leave Oregon and go where I could get Christian fellowship. So I packed my belongings and drove down to Southern California."

When Kathy arrived at Calvary Chapel with her young daughter, they suggested she stay at the Lord's House, a nearby Christian house run by people from the church. By accident Gary and I had managed to end up on the street where the Lord's House was located. But then, somehow, we all felt it hadn't been an accident.

Chapter Thirteen
Doing Time

I was now about four weeks old in the Lord. It had been quite a while since I had seen Paul. After he left Silverado Canyon, he had gone to live in St. Louis. He came out to the west coast, and when we got together he was surprised to hear I had become a Christian. He seemed to be struggling in his own relationship with the Lord and I did my best to encourage him.

We went to a Bible study together that Chuck Smith was leading in the tent. We were a little late, so we had to go down to the front and sit in the aisle on the ground.

Chuck looked down at me and said, ''Bruce, would you like to come up here and share your testimony?''

My mind did a quick flip-flop. I had never been able to speak in front of crowds, and there were at least two thousand people packed into the tent. As I stood up, my brain fogged up. I don't remember what I said, but I shared for ten or fifteen minutes.

When I came down, Paul had a big smile on his face. His faith had been encouraged by my conversion. The next day he left to go back to St. Louis, so I didn't see him for a while.

One night at the Margarette House, we began to pray for one another's needs. Everyone in the room knew I was scheduled to appear in the state courthouse the following day. Someone prayed God would move into the courtroom and touch the judge's heart. He prayed God would work a miracle and not send me to prison.

After we had finished praying and were sitting around, one of the brothers told me, "Bruce, the Lord spoke to my heart. You're not going to go to prison. You might do some jail time, but you're not gonna be sent away to prison."

I was hoping what he said was true, but I knew the chances were slim. Almost all the other people arrested for sales to state agents had gone to court and everyone had received long prison sentences. I was going to plead guilty, and the public defender had told me I could expect a sentence of about three to five years! Then I still faced the federal bust and the two possession charges.

Early the next day, a friend drove Gary and me to the Superior Courthouse in Santa Ana. Arriving early, we stood in the hallway and waited for the courtroom doors to open. In the crowded corridor stood an old friend from grade school days.

We exchanged greetings, and the conversation shifted to my conversion from drugs. As I shared my new life, my friend showed real interest and nodded agreement to each point I made. But we were interrupted and separated when the courtroom doors opened and those in the corridor began to move through the doorways. Gary and I sat next to Nam. While the room was settling, I stepped up and quizzed my public defender.

"I talked to the DA," he said. "They're going to lower the charges against you because of your guilty plea. You'll only do a couple of years and will probably even get more time off for good behavior."

"That's all right. Whatever they do is fine."

I sat back down and began to share Christ with Nam. I handed him a tract, but he gave me a disgusted look.

"Hey, that's not gonna help me any. What I need is a good lawyer."

"Look, Bill, give your life to Christ. He's the best lawyer you can get."

"Well, you're going to prison, too. I don't see God getting you out of trouble."

"Well . . . I'm trusting God to help me, but no matter what happens in this courtroom, Christ will be with me."

Bill was not too receptive, so I let the subject drop. Court was called into session and for several hours one defendant after another was called forward. The presiding judge was supposed to be the toughest in the district. I watched him sentence everyone to sentences of five years up to life—and most hadn't done anything compared to me!

My name was finally called. The district attorney read the charges against me. I was scared. A million thoughts ran through my brain. The words of that Christian brother flashed into my head—" 'You're not going to go to prison.' Prison: I wonder what it will be like. How will my parents feel knowing their son is in the state penitentiary?"

When the DA finished reading the charges, the judge asked if I had anything to say.

"No, your Honor."

"How do you plead?"

"Guilty to all charges, your Honor."

The judge looked at me for a moment, deep in thought. "I don't know why, but something is telling me to give you another chance. I sentence you to three years in the state penitentiary, but I'm suspending that sentence and placing you on three years' formal probation. The terms are that you do two months in Orange County Jail, abstain from drugs, and keep out of any kind of trouble.''

I couldn't believe my ears! I was ecstatic, and was shouting, "Praise the Lord!" within my heart.

Gary was jumping up and down in his seat. Nam seemed in shock. My public defender and the DA had looks of disbelief on their faces. The judge's sudden change of heart had surprised everyone.

As I walked out of the courtroom I smiled at Nam and said, "The Lord can help you." He smiled back weakly, but there was no time to talk.

Gary and I returned to Margarette House and told everyone the amazing news. We all realized the judge's decision had been a miracle.

I had to turn myself in to the Orange County Jail several days later to begin serving the two-month sentence the judge had imposed. Although I knew I might not be released after two months because of the pending federal trial, I still possessed a strong peace. This time there was no need to smuggle drugs in. Psychologically, I was at peace. I had Jesus, and he would give the strength and stamina to handle whatever was ahead.

As I was booked in, the opportunity to share Christ with each of the deputies availed itself. It always seemed natural to talk of my relationship with the Lord and how he had given me a new life. I could tell they were surprised to hear about Jesus from me.

When they led me into the cellblock, all of my previous jail experiences began to come to mind. I was reminded of the violence, perversion, and boredom. I began to question why this was happening to me.

"Wait a minute," I thought. "What is God's will? God has given me a purpose for living—to share the gospel. Wherever he puts me is his will."

When you are a Christian, there is no such thing as an accident. I was here for a reason; there was someone here God wanted me to reach. I was also certain this experience would discipline and build character in me—even if it became painful.

They assigned me to a four-man cell. Immediately I became acquainted with each of my new cell mates. On the opposite bunk was a hippie named Gary who had a full beard and hair to his waist. He was in jail for selling grass.

The bunk above Gary was occupied by Nido, a well-built, full-blooded Indian. Although he was only eighteen, Nido had spent a great deal of time in confinement. He was currently in for a stabbing. He was violent, especially when loaded on reds, and was considered one of the "tough guys" in the cellblock.

On the bunk below me was Harold, a thirty-five-year-old who weighed close to 300 pounds. Harold soon began to worry me. He was intelligent, but was often depressed or in a bad mood. He punched on me to release tension, and I was always afraid he would lose his temper.

After I had met everyone, I sat back on my bunk and talked to the Lord. "Wow, Lord, how am I gonna tell these guys about you? This is a different world. They're not going to be interested in what I have to say. You're gonna have to work out some way to get me started."

I sat on my bunk reading my Bible, hoping someone would ask me what I was reading. Witnessing here would be different from anything on the outside.

The next day was Sunday, and I was excited about attending a chapel service. I had enjoyed chapel as a non-Christian because it provided an opportunity to escape my cell and talk to friends from other cellblocks. This time I was interested in the service itself. I wanted to meet the chaplain and have fellowship with him.

On Sunday morning, half our module went to chapel. There were at least 150 prisoners in the service. The chaplain gave a good Bible message, then finished with a question.

"Has the Lord done anything for any of you men?" No one said anything; he repeated his question. "Has Christ done anything for any of you men?"

I told myself it wasn't important to stand and say anything here. "Besides," I thought, "who would listen to me anyway?" This was only my second day in jail and I was afraid of what everyone would think. But deep inside, I knew God wanted me to stand and share. The chaplain continued.

"Christ said, 'Whosoever, therefore, shall confess me before men, him will I confess also before my Father, who is in heaven. But whosoever shall deny me before men, him will I also deny before my Father, who is in heaven.' "

My hand shot up. Christ's words pierced my heart.

I stood and quickly shared my drug background, how I had become a Christian, and how my life had been changed by the Lord. I talked for ten minutes.

"Praise God!" the chaplain exclaimed, as I sat down. My testimony had encouraged him, but I wondered how the prisoners would respond.

"Lord, they know. There won't be any more games now."

As we walked back to our cells, I expected rejection. But several prisoners introduced themselves and said they appreciated what I said. That one chapel service opened many opportunities to share my faith. Even my cell mates began to notice I was always reading my Bible.

"Don't you do anything but read that book?" they would ask. "You have to read that thing all the time?"

"I don't have to, but I really enjoy it. It contains lots of interesting things."

Still very young in the faith, I was soaking in all of God's promises. I claimed each verse in which he offered something. The passages in which Jesus promised joy, peace, and love made my outlook brighter as I claimed them for myself.

Nido figured if I spent so much time reading the Bible, I must know something. "What about the heathen in Africa? Is God gonna send them to hell when they haven't even heard about Jesus?"

"I think there is an answer to that in the book of Romans. Yes, here it is. It says in Romans chapter one that the whole world is guilty before God, because even nature reveals God exists. All men are born with a knowledge of right and wrong. If man deviates from his own moral code, he judges himself. That's how the heathen in Africa will be judged. They will be judged by what they do with their knowledge, because all men are guilty before God.

When you stand before God, the issue will not be what happens to the heathen, but what you did with Jesus Christ. If you don't accept him, you'll have no excuse."

God kept revealing the correct passages to me for each question I was asked. I was always able to find a key Scripture to answer their questions. God was faithful.

On one occasion we stayed up all night and talked about the Bible. I talked for twelve hours. I tried my best not to irritate the inmates in other cells, but my cell mates kept asking questions all night long. Occasionally a prisoner from another cell would yell out, "Shut up, you Jesus freak!"

However, some prisoners were listening carefully. In the cell next to ours were two Christians who were out of touch with God. They rededicated their lives to the Lord that night and we began to have fellowship the next day through the bars. I was excited about the warm fellowship we were able to have. It was like coming upon an oasis in the desert.

In spite of this victory, Harold began to attack me hostilely. H e was anti-God, anti-Bible, and anti-me. Often he grabbed my shirt and breathed threats at me. "I'm gonna kill you, you Christian!" he would yell. Then he would let go. I wasn't certain if Harold would try to kill me or not. I was constantly in prayer for him.

Gary was a little easier to talk to. He argued about philosophical issues, because he had been raised as a Unitarian. One evening I told Gary that Jesus is God. That statement sent the cell into a turmoil. It was easy for everyone to accept Jesus as a good man, but to think of him as God was unacceptable. They realized if Christ was God they would be forced to make some kind of a decision. You can't accept Jesus as God and then ignore him.

That night my cell mates tossed and turned in their bunks. I was sharing almost constantly, and these men were receiving as much exposure to Christianity as most people receive in a lifetime. I could tell the verses I had shown about the deity of Christ had hit the mark. They were all under conviction, but their pride was keeping them from making a decision.

After that first chapel service, I met the chaplain in his office. Although he was much older than I, we immediately had close Christian fellowship. He was elated by my testimony and love for Christ. Very few prisoners love the Lord.

The chaplain asked me to write out my testimony for those praying for his jail ministry. I told him I would compose the letter, and asked if he would write a character letter to the federal judge handling my upcoming trial. It is standard procedure for defendants to have friends send in letters evaluating their character. The chaplain was the only person I could ask, and he agreed to send in a letter. Before I left his office, the chaplain gave me all the Christian literature I could use.

Once a week the prisoners were taken on the roof for exercise. The roof had a fenced enclosure six stories above ground with volleyball and basketball courts, as well as areas where the inmates could talk to prisoners from other cellblocks.

Once on the roof, I sat down with the two Christians from the cell next to mine. They were excited about living for the Lord and were beginning to talk to other prisoners about Christ. They brought several non-Christians to talk to me.

"I went to Calvary Chapel a couple of times," said Bob, one of their friends. "But nothing happened to me. I have a lot of Christian friends, but I'm really not sure I want to become one myself."

I showed Bob several verses that had become meaningful to me. I read Second Peter 3:9, "The Lord is not slack concerning his promise, as some men count slackness, but is longsuffering toward us, not willing that any should perish, but that all should come to repentance."

I shared how Christ fulfilled Bible prophecy and how he is coming back soon. Bob was responsive to what I shared, and the next day, he raised his hand in a chapel service to indicate he wanted to become a Christian.

During the Christmas season, a special announcement was made that Calvary Chapel was going to present the chapel service. When I heard the news, I started telling everyone to go.

"Man, you're crazy. I never go to chapel," one guy told me.

"This is gonna be different. I know you'll dig this. It will be different from any church you've ever been to."

A large number attended the service, but we sat for twenty minutes waiting for the group to show up. Finally, Tom Stipe, Rick Nabors, and Greg Laurie came into the chapel and began to make their presentation. They sang and shared their testimonies and I could tell the freshness of the program made a positive impact on the prisoners.

After the service I went over to talk to Rick. A

deputy jumped between us. I'm certain he thought we were going to pass drugs or some other contraband.

When we were back in our cells, our module hummed. The gospel had been presented so well almost everyone was talking about the service. I later found out from the chaplain that six men had come to Christ as a result of that short program.

Chapter Fourteen
Six Years in Prison!

Harold and Nido agreed it was impressive that the state sales charges had been dismissed, but they claimed it was simple luck. "Now if you go free on the two possession charges, and the federal sales bust, *that* will be a miracle," Nido told me. "If that happens, it will definitely be from God, and even I'll become a Christian."

"Yeah," Harold chimed in caustically, "if you get out of all those charges, I'll become a Christian too."

"You guys better be careful," I cautioned, "God just may let me off so you will believe."

"Yeah," Harold replied sarcastically, "I'll believe it when I see it."

I prayed that night asking God to show Harold and Nido some sign he was real. I tried not to pray selfishly, asking him to save me from prison. I wanted God's will in my life—whatever that would mean.

One morning I was taken to the Westminster courthouse to appear on the first drug possession charge. While I was in the holding cell below the courthouse, the public defender came down and informed me that charges had been dismissed. "Wow, Lord, thank you again," I prayed as they transported me back to the Orange County Jail.

A few days later I was taken to the Fullerton courthouse to appear on the second possession charge. Again the public defender came down to the holding tank.

"I don't understand this. They dismissed all the charges against you. Do you have some connections?"

I had connections, but they weren't with the court. I marveled how God had motivated the authorities to drop the charges. In both cases I was as good as convicted. Why had the courts had a sudden change of heart? I could only say, "Thank you, Jesus."

In addition to these offenses, Santa Barbara County had a hold on me, so I could not be released until I appeared in that courthouse for a trespassing fine I had never paid. My parents drove north and straightened out the problem. They paid a $100 fine for me.

"Bruce, it's heavy you got out of so much prison time," Nido said, "but this federal rap is gonna be different. They're gonna nail you on this one."

"I'm just trusting the Lord, Nido. I never claimed he would get me out of anything. He may want me to serve time in the federal pen. On the other hand, he has the power to free me if he wants to."

"I'll believe it when I see it," Harold added bitterly.

Christmas was approaching, and I remembered being in jail three years earlier. How different things were now! Some prisoners couldn't understand how I could be so happy with a federal rap hanging over my head.

"I don't care where I'm at, as long as I'm in God's will. The purpose of my life is to know God better, and that's all that matters to me."

Everyone is lonely in jail. Few prisoners really get close to each other, and the tough guys are usually the most insecure. When Christmas comes, it is amazing how depressed most inmates become. I could now give genuine comfort to other prisoners because of the depth of my relationship with God.

The night before my federal court appearance, I began to get edgy. A large monster seemed to be on my horizon, threatening to take away my peace of mind. I reaffirmed to God that whatever he did would be okay with me.

The next morning an Orange County sheriff came to transport me to the federal courthouse in Los Angeles. He had to be familiar with the case against me because officers read up on the prisoners they transport.

"Hi," I said, climbing into the patrol car. The officer was stone faced. He didn't respond in any way.

The gate to the jail opened and we drove into the city. A happy feeling swept over me. "Boy, this is sure a beautiful day, isn't it?"

The officer made no response. He must have felt it would be wrong to make small talk with me.

"I've really been looking forward to this trip to court. I want to get this thing out of the way." I didn't think the sheriff was listening, but I had to express my heart. "Whatever happens, I know the judge's decision will be the best thing for me."

The officer looked at me. "Do you think you're going to be convicted?" he asked finally.

"I don't know. But whatever happens will be God's will."

That statement caused the officer to open up. He smiled for the first time and asked, "Why do you feel it will be God's will?"

As we traveled down the Santa Ana Freeway, I shared my background and personal testimony. He was very receptive and asked a number of probing questions. Before we entered the courthouse, he bought me lunch. Everywhere I went the deputy had to go with me and I talked constantly about Jesus. I could tell he believed I was trustworthy because he kept a loose watch over me once we were in the courthouse.

I was fingerprinted, photographed, and placed in the large jail cell in the basement. "What are you here for?" one man asked.

"Drug sales," I replied.

"Man, that's bad. They're hanging all pushers."

I was able to shift the conversation to my conversion experience. I knew most people would respond well to my testimony.

After a few hours, I was taken up to the courtroom. As the sheriff and I walked through the corridor, people stared at me. My wrists were handcuffed together, and a chain ran around my waist. Everyone must have wondered what heinous crime I had committed.

My mother was in the courtroom. Her eyes were

red, and she was obviously depressed. I reminded myself what my past life had done to her and Dad.

The courtroom was huge. The walls were marble, and a giant eagle stared at us from behind the judge. It was different from the courtrooms I had seen before. It looked like a set from the FBI television program.

My public defender informed me that because I was pleading guilty to all charges, they would not be hard on me. He said I could expect six years in prison. "Six years!" I thought, "what a long time. Lord, can I make it through all those years?"

The courtroom was called to order. The district attorney began to read all the charges against me. By the time the DA was finished. I looked like a hardened criminal. He hadn't missed anything. He told about the drownings and said it was my fault.

"Do you have anything to say for yourself?" asked the judge.

"No, your Honor, I don't."

"How do you plead?"

"I plead guilty. Guilty to all charges."

"I sentence you to six years in the federal penitentiary."

I returned to my seat, numbed. Six years was a light sentence for all I had done; I had expected twenty years. But even so, I wondered if I could handle it. My mind was having a difficult time accepting the sentence. I had hoped for a miracle.

"Well, Lord, I guess that's it. You know what I can handle. You must want me in prison to witness. But, Lord, I sure think I could be more effective on the outside."

Sitting in front of a judge is a traumatic experience.

I imagined how awesome it would be to sit in front of God and have him judge you—especially if you had never asked Jesus to cleanse your heart from sin.

I turned to see my mother crying uncontrollably. She stood and left the courtroom. The bailiff walked to the bench and handed the judge some papers. He leafed through them for several moments and seemed deep in thought.

The judge called me back up in front. "Bruce," he said, "are you sure you don't have anything to say on your own behalf?"

"Well," I said, "my life has been changed. Just recently I became a Christian." I quickly told him the major things that had happened in my life.

"What should I do with you?" the judge asked.

"Well . . . I feel I would do society more good outside than I would in prison. What I've done is wrong, and I deserve to go to prison, but my life has really changed, and I don't take drugs anymore. In fact, I have encouraged my friends to stop taking drugs too."

"I have thirteen letters in front of me that say your life has changed," said the judge. "But it would be a great injustice if I let you go back into society. Every time you've been in trouble, you've been set free. Now you're in worse trouble. You've destroyed people's lives. But it would also be a great injustice to send you to prison if you have really changed. Bruce . . . I'm going to give you one more chance. But I affirm by the power invested in me, if you ever get arrested again, I'll make certain you do many years in the federal penitentiary. I'm suspending your sentence and placing you on probation. You will do two months in the county jail on weekends. I don't want to be too easy on you, but if you're sincere, you'll make it through those 30 weekends.''

"Praise the Lord!" I couldn't believe what God had done. Gordon, the agent who had arrested me, seemed pleased by the verdict. The deputy sheriff who brought me in from Orange County Jail had a big smile on his face. When we left the courtroom, he told me he had prayed for me.

In the corridor, I saw my mother's tear-stained face. The deputy gave me permission to talk to her. I threw my arms around Mom and we embraced emotionally.

"Why are you smiling?" she asked between sobs.

"Mom, I'm free! I don't have to go to prison! The judge suspended my sentence and I only have to do two months in jail." Mom began to cry even harder, but now they were tears of joy.

On the way back to the jail, the deputy and I had a good conversation. "You really got off easy. With all the things you did, you were really lucky the judge let you off."

"It's a miracle from God," I replied. "There's no other way to explain it. Especially when you consider the Lord got me out of the other charges too."

I was excited about returning to jail so I could tell my cell mates what God had done. I knew they couldn't refute this miracle. What could they do now but believe? As I entered the cubicle, each facial expression revealed the judge's decision. That "I told you so" look was on every face.

I decided to play with their curiosity. Crossing the cell, I flopped out on my bunk as if nothing important had happened. Anxious expressions colored every face.

"Well?" Nido asked, waiting.

"What happened, man?" Harold blurted out. "Tell us!"

"Oh . . . " I said casually, "I have to do some more time."

"I knew it," Nido smiled in relief.

"What did I tell you," Harold laughed. "How much time you got to do?"

"Oh . . . I have to do two more."

"Two more years?"

"No, just two more months."

"You're kidding. You didn't get any prison time?"

"Nope, only two months, which I'll do on weekends."

"Man, I can't believe that," Nido replied exasperatedly. "How did you pull it off?"

"I didn't do anything. The Lord got me off again. I told you guys God really answers prayer. I prayed God would show you a sign, and he did! All I can say is praise the Lord!"

"That's too much," Nido said.

"Okay, you gonna accept the Lord now?"

Nido and Harold looked at each other, then down at the floor. They had worked themselves into a corner.

"Ah . . . well, maybe," Nido faltered.

"No . . . not yet," Harold stammered.

My cell mates were under tremendous conviction, but their pride was keeping them from making a decision for Christ.

I had only a week left on my sentence. Each night as I read my Bible, Nido would ask me to read to him. When I read out loud, I always selected an evangelistic passage for my friends.

As my release drew near, I realized my friends

were not going to accept Christ. I prayed that some-day the seeds which had been planted in their hearts would bring fruit.

I was released on Christmas Day. For the first time in seven years I was looking forward to being with my parents. Through the drug years, family ties had lost their meaning, but now I strongly desired to be close to my family. Mom and Dad welcomed me home warmly. We all rejoiced that I didn't have to go to prison.

I began praying more earnestly for my parents. I felt burdened for the whole world, but was especially anxious that Mom and Dad come to Christ. It was difficult to live with the knowledge they were not Christians.

At every opportunity I gave God glory for keeping me out of prison. My parents insisted I had been very lucky.

"No, Mom and Dad, the Lord worked a miracle."

"Well, I guess it is a miracle, Bruce," my mother replied. "You know we've always loved God. We tried hard to raise you the best way we knew how."

"I know, Mom, and I really appreciate everything you and Dad have done for me. Not many parents would have stuck by me like you did. I just want you to know Jesus in the same way I know him. I want you to be born again. Would you and Dad come to church with me this Sunday?"

"We have our own church, Bruce."

"You haven't gone to church in years. Why don't you come down to Calvary with me?"

"Okay, Bruce, we'll go, but just this once."

We all went to church that Sunday. As we ap-proached the tent I could tell they were having some reservations, but after we entered and heard Pastor Chuck Smith give his Sunday morning message, I could see they were moved.

"That was really nice," my mom said on the way home. "It was so different from what I expected."

My parents began attending regularly. I tried to answer their many questions, but it was difficult because I was their son.

One night I took my mother to an evening Bible study. When the altar call was given at the end of the service, she went forward to become a Christian. I was ecstatic. It was difficult to contain my feelings. My mother had given her life to Christ!

I concentrated my prayers on Dad. Pastor Chuck's ministry was having an influence on his life, but for some reason he just didn't make a decision.

One afternoon I called home, and my father answered the phone. Instead of answering, "Hello," he answered with a bright "Praise the Lord!" I knew immediately something had happened.

Dad shared how he had been witnessing to different people on his delivery stops. He wanted to tell other people about Christ. I knew he had become a Christian. He had opened his heart to the Lord!

Although I had already served two months on my state sales conviction, Nam had still not been sentenced. He was in county jail and I went to see him several times.

"Look, Bill, I'm not saying if you accept the Lord, you'll get out of prison like I did, but whatever happens it will be better for you."

"Yeah, yeah. There are a lot of different ways to reach God. Meditation, Buddhism, yoga. Don't try to tell me you have to be a Christian to reach God. I just don't want to hear it."

"Listen, Bill, I'm telling you Christ will take care of your problems. He's the only way—"

"I'm sorry," he interrupted, "I'm just not interested. Look, man, if you really want to help, put a gun in the courtroom."

"No. I'd never do that. No way."

After the conversation had changed subjects several times, Nam asked if I would pick him up at the courthouse after he was sentenced.

"Wait a minute. You're not getting released."

"Look," he said in a whisper. "All you have to do is leave a car in front of the courthouse. Just leave it sittin' there with the keys in it."

"No, Bill, I'm not gonna do it. I just can't get involved in anything like that."

I didn't go to see Nam get sentenced, but I read about it in the newspaper. He had been on the eighth floor of the courthouse building when he tried an escape. He jumped the railing, ran through the spectators section, and out the doors. With deputies chasing, he sprinted down eight flights of stairs and out into the parking lot where some friends had left a car. As he struggled to start it, the officers caught up and dragged him back into the courthouse at gunpoint. He was later sentenced to five years in a maximum security prison.

After Bill was put in San Quentin, he sent me a postcard with a picture of Jesus on it. He wrote that finally he was trusting the Lord. He wanted my prayers so he could make it through all those years in prison. I praised God that Bill had finally turned to Christ.

Chapter Fifteen
The Birdman

I moved into an apartment across the street from Calvary. Rick Nabors was my roommate, and we studied the Word together when our schedules permitted. Because we lived so close to the church, it was easy to attend many of the evening Bible studies.

The terms for my federal probation declared I must have a full-time job. I hired on at a construction company and worked a five-day week. It was my first steady job.

Each Saturday morning I was required to turn myself in to the Theo Lacy branch of the Orange County Jail. After spending the weekend in confinement, I was released Sunday night at 6:00. I had been sentenced to serve two months in jail—a total of thirty weekends in all.

When I turned myself in that first weekend, I entered the main gate and was searched for illegal contraband. They sent me to a clothing change area, where my street clothes were exchanged for levis, tennis shoes, and a blue work shirt with "Orange County Theo Lacy" stamped on the back. I was given a bedroll and assigned a bunk in a barracks which contained 100 men. The bedding area was open and nothing would keep me from talking with other prisoners. There were no bars anywhere.

Weekend prisoners can't go to chapel services. Except for work assignments, we were allowed only in the library or our barracks. Because we had freedom to walk about and meet other prisoners, I knew there would be many opportunities to witness.

That first Saturday morning, I noticed a black prisoner on the other side of the dorm reading his Bible. Overjoyed, I walked across the room to his bunk.

"Hey, are you a Christian?

"Yeah, are you?"

"Praise the Lord, I sure am. How long have you been saved?"

"Just a couple of weeks. I became a Christian by reading my Bible."

"That's neat. My name's Bruce, what's yours?"

"Clayton's my name."

I was able to answer many of Clayton's questions about the Bible. We started to read and discuss the Word on his bunk, and I became aware that other inmates were leaning in our direction, attempting to hear what we were saying.

Prisoners began to ask questions about the Bible. Before I knew what had happened, Clayton and I were in the center of a little Bible study. The following weekend, some of these men invited Christ into their lives. We quickly developed a nucleus of Christians and began meeting each week.

I asked some of the inmates if they would like to come to church. Monday night at Calvary included music and a good evangelistic message from pastor Chuck Smith. Four or five weekenders came with me and several went forward at the invitation.

So many prisoners were now sitting around my bunk for our Bible studies, the guards began to take notice. I could understand their concern because riots happen quickly in jail. On several occasions the guards asked why everyone was congregating around my bunk. When I told them we were having Bible studies, they laughed.

"Are you sure you're not smuggling drugs into our jail?"

"I don't take drugs anymore; I'm a Christian."

"That's what everybody says. Nobody takes drugs anymore."

When I came into the jail each weekend they searched me more thoroughly. They also woke me up in the middle of the night to search for drugs. They didn't find anything and must eventually have realized my popularity was caused by Jesus, not by drugs.

Theo Lacy Jail had several work programs. Sometimes we were sent to a car wash in downtown Santa Ana to clean the county's vehicles. At Orange County Hospital we did general grounds work: hoeing weeds, raking up leaves, and cutting lawns. We were often sent to clean up state or county property. We would cut down weeds on the side of a freeway, or spend hours picking up trash at some park.

One of the worst assignments was the dog pound. Inmates were responsible both for cleaning cages and putting dogs to death. All the prisoners hated that job. The guards asked for volunteers, but no one would ever respond. They never forced anyone to kill dogs, but they could make life difficult for anyone who wouldn't.

The kitchen was another assignment. Hours were long and the work constant, but you had all the food you could eat. Potatoes are served at almost every jail meal, and I must have peeled 20,000 of them.

While cutting weeds at the county courthouse, I

met a prisoner named Mike. We were sitting on the lawn at lunch when he told me why I shouldn't eat white bread. Mike was a health fanatic and had traded his sandwich to another prisoner for extra fruit.

"That stuff will give you cancer," Mike said, then proceeded to tell me why.

I didn't doubt the truth of what he said, but saw an opportunity to share my faith. "If I get cancer, Christ can heal me. God has the power both to heal me and keep me from getting sick. Besides, the Bible clearly states in the last days men will try to make other men abstain from certain foods. God created all foods to be received with thanksgiving."

I believed in good nutrition, but it was not nearly as important as it had been. Mike was disgusted because I wasn't deeply into nutrition and he didn't think too much of people who were into Jesus.

The next weekend, on the Saturday before Easter, I met Mike again in the dorm. He was high. "I believe marijuana is peace. It's God's gift to man."

Mike had a drug background similar to mine. His full name was Mike Byrd and he was known in the drug culture as the "Birdman of La Habra." He produced hash oil and had a reputation for making the best. A big dealer, he had been busted only for possession with the intent to sell and was doing five weekends.

We engaged in a discussion about drugs and God, but it seemed fruitless. When I began to witness to another prisoner, Mike interrupted to give his personal opinion.

"Jesus was a good man. He was a man of the truth."

160

"Now wait a minute. Either Jesus Christ was the greatest liar in the world, the biggest deceiver, and the biggest phony—or he was God."

"What do you mean?" he said.

"Well, Jesus said, 'Before Abraham was, I AM.' "

"That doesn't even make sense. What do you mean?"

"It's in the Gospel of John," I answered. "Jesus claimed he had always existed. No good man would make such a claim. Have you ever read the Gospel of John?"

"Sure."

"Well, then you know Jesus is God's Son." Mike didn't seem familiar with the book, and I had a feeling he had never read it. "Look Mike, if you're serious about knowing who Jesus is, he'll reveal himself to you. Tonight when you go to bed, read the Gospel of John with an open heart and ask Jesus to reveal himself to you."

When I went to bed, I prayed that God would bind Satan's power and open Mike's eyes. The Holy Spirit's influence had been so strong in our conversation, I knew God was going to do something powerful.

Next morning, on Easter Sunday, Mike came to my bed and woke me up.

"Bruce," he said humbly, "Jesus *is* the Lord."

"Well, praise God!" I could already see a difference in Mike's appearance. A broad smile was on his lips and his countenance radiated the peace of God. There was no doubt in my mind he had been born again.

After breakfast, Mike came up beaming. "Why

did you tell me to read the book of John?''

"It was the Holy Spirit. God knew what you needed.''

Mike and I spent the day studying the Word. He had all kinds of questions. "How could God come into the world?'' he asked.

"If you wanted to communicate to ants, the best way would be to become an ant. That's how God communicated with men.''

"Wow, that's neat.''

He continued to ask questions, and by the Spirit's power, I turned to different passages in the Scriptures to satisfy him. He was as hungry for spiritual things as any new Christian I'd ever seen.

When we were being released that evening, we were both floating. One of the guards scrutinized Mike's grinning face in the inspection line.

"What are you smiling about?'' he asked gruffly.

"I'm just happy.''

As we walked out the door, Mike turned back to the guard and said, "God bless you.''

The officer developed a quizzical expression on his face. "Why? I didn't sneeze!''

"I guess that was a dumb thing to say,'' Mike commented in the parking lot.

"Come over to my car; I want to give you some tracts. I'll give you my phone number too.''

After I had given him the literature and my phone number, we shook hands and said good-bye. Mike drove off with his wife. Three days later he called from his apartment in La Habra.

"Bruce, I need help. I'm having trouble.''

I laughed. "That was to be expected. That's what happens when you become a Christian. Satan starts hitting you. Mike, you've got to trust the Lord with all your heart and mind. You don't need to talk to me, you need to talk to God."

"Listen, Bruce, I *really* need help. Can I come over?"

"Okay," I said finally. I could tell he wasn't pulling out of his depression. I gave Mike directions to my house and he said he'd be right down. Several hours passed, and when he didn't arrive, I guessed he had decided against coming. Then the phone rang.

"Bruce, you'll never guess what happened. You gave me the wrong directions. When I couldn't find your house, I went to the Bible study at Calvary. You know what the minister said? He said, 'Our problem is we go to men, not God, when we have problems.' I think God has given me the answers."

"That's great. I knew God would meet your needs. Now that you're in the area, why don't you come over and we can have some fellowship."

I gave Mike better directions, and he drove over. I could tell by the look on his face God had taken care of everything. He shared that his wife had gone out with another man.

"That is heavy. But you have to trust the Lord. Don't let this situation get you down. Keep looking to Christ and learn from him."

Mike's problems still existed, but he had learned to trust the Lord. We prayed together for wisdom in dealing with the situation.

When we arrived at Theo Lacy that weekend, we were both ready to witness to the other inmates. I continued to teach Mike things that would help him in his walk with the Lord. Teaching him gave both of us tremendous opportunities. As I answered his questions, many others became interested. Invariably, some non-Christian would start asking questions and end up becoming a Christian.

Many of the jail's tough guys mocked us, but you could tell they were also secretly listening. I knew why. We weren't talking about religion, we were talking about a personal relationship with God. We shared why we were going to heaven. They had probably never heard this message before.

Mike's fifth weekend ended, and he was released for good. I hated to see him leave, but he continued to attend Calvary every week. With Mike gone, I decided to spend more time in the library, the only place I could contact prisoners from other barracks.

One Saturday I met a man named Bill who had just become a Jehovah's Witness. He seemed to have many honest questions when I shared my faith.

"If what you say is the truth, why do the Jehovah's Witnesses hold a different view?" he asked.

"Listen Bill, it doesn't matter what I say, or what they say, or what any man says. It's what God says. If you're not born again, no matter which church you go to, you're not going to heaven."

"Well, I love the Lord," he replied defensively.

"You can love the Lord and still not have life. You've got to be born again. God has to put a new Spirit—his Spirit—in your heart."

I showed Bill the third chapter of John and he saw with his own eyes what I had told him was true. A week later, I could tell God was dealing with his heart.

"I want to get born again, Bruce."

We prayed together and Bill's name was written in the Book of Life. Later, with the discernment only

164

God gives, he was able to see the Watchtower Society a little more clearly.

"You know, Bruce, when we read the Bible at Kingdom Hall, they always interpreted what we read. What I thought it said and what they claimed it meant were always two different things. I felt uneasy about what they said, but I didn't know if it was true because I had never gone to any other church."

Most of the questions Bill asked were about Jehovah's Witness doctrine. I shared the many passages of Scripture which prove Jesus is indeed God in the flesh, not *a god!* Bill was told it was wrong to worship Jesus. So I showed him John 20:28, where even the Jehovah's Witness Bible shows Thomas worshiped Jesus and called him God. We spent hours comparing the doctrines the Witnesses teach with Scripture.

Bill went to Kingdom Hall the next week and caused so much trouble he was excommunicated from the cult. He asked so many questions they couldn't handle, they finally forbade him to come back.

Bill's wife was also a Witness, and soon she too became a Christian. When Bill's weekends were over, both he and his wife began to attend a Bible-believing church in northern Orange County.

I was now working for a uniform and supply company during the week. The job consisted of delivering uniforms and rags to Los Angeles and San Fernando. I drove a large truck and carried hundreds of dollars by the end of the day. The job turned out to be very good experience. As my first long-term work experience, it provided money for expenses and allowed me to build my savings.

I made deliveries for ten hours and was just barely

able to make it to church each night. My eyes were almost always bloodshot at Calvary because I was so exhausted. It was often difficult to keep from falling asleep, but I was so hungry for the Word, I managed to stay awake by the grace of God.

Because I was alone in my truck each day, I was able to talk to the Lord between deliveries. On the freeway, I would sing songs to the Lord. Every minute of my work day was enjoyable. I was meeting all types of people and was able to witness at most of my stops.

Each week I delivered at a tire company in North Hollywood. I dreaded the backroom of that establishment, because the walls were completely covered with pornography. It was difficult to avoid seeing some of those blatant photographs each time I entered the shop.

Before walking into that room I asked the Lord for total victory. I claimed the blood of Christ and asked him to blind my eyes. I wanted my mind on Jesus when I entered that building. God answered that prayer and I found complete relief from lustful thoughts.

One day I drove past the headquarters of a Jewish-Christian evangelism organization in Glendale. I stopped in and talked with one of the staff members.

"Here," he said as I departed. "Why don't you take a few of our tracts written to Jews. They might come in handy in your jail ministry."

"That's neat. Thanks a lot."

As I stepped into the van, I looked through the leaflets. Most were written by converted rabbis and looked convincing to me. But I couldn't imagine

166

using them, because I just didn't know any Jews. After work, I deposited them in the glove compartment of my car.

That weekend, an unusual character named Doug was assigned to the bunk next to mine. All he could do was talk about himself. Among other things he claimed to be a black belt in karate, a perfect marksman, a jet pilot, and several other unbelievable claims. Whenever he was away from his bunk, the other prisoners would savagely make fun of him. I couldn't help feeling sorry for Doug. I began to pray for an opportunity to share with him. My eye caught sight of a star of David hanging around his neck.

"Are you a Jew?" I asked.

"Yeah, why?"

"Oh, that's neat. I've been wanting to talk to a Jew for a long time."

"What?"

"I'm a Christian. I'm a Jesus freak, and I've been wanting to talk to a Jew for a long time. I believe firmly the Jews are still God's chosen people."

We began to converse about Doug's cultural heritage, and I had no trouble convincing him to talk about himself. He came from an orthodox Jewish family but no longer practiced the religion.

We talked all night. I shared every Old Testament prophecy I could think of which Christ fulfilled. I turned to Isaiah 53 and showed how the Messiah would suffer for the sins of the world. I turned to Psalm 22 which describes exactly how the Messiah would die. Then I turned to the New Testament and read how Jesus had fulfilled each prophecy. I showed him at least fifteen different prophecies before I was through.

"Do you know what the numerical chances are for Jesus to fulfill *one* of these prophecies by accident? About a hundred to one! But Jesus fulfilled over three hundred different prophecies. The odds he could have done it by accident are astronomical."

"That's really heavy," Doug said matter-of-factly, but he didn't respond from the heart. He knew what I said was true, but he simply didn't care.

When we finally retired, I prayed for Doug. He was the first Jew I had ever talked to about Christ and I kept thinking of the words of Paul, "to the Jew first and then to the Greek." This man was one of the chosen people, but he no longer cared about God. I identified Doug with all other Jews and felt a tremendous burden for his soul.

On Sunday morning I asked, "Would you like to have Jesus as your Messiah?"

"No," he answered rather casually.

"Tonight, before you go to sleep, ask God if Jesus is his Son. He is the Messiah and he came to give you life."

Doug showed no indication he would do as I asked, so I continued to pray silently for him. That evening when we were released, I asked if he would talk for a moment.

"Come over to my car. I've got some things I'd like to give you."

I reached into my glove compartment and pulled out the tracts the Hebrew Christian had given me.

"Here. If you want to know if everything I've said is true, read these tracts. You've spent thousands of hours studying for school; it will be worth it to spend a few minutes reading these leaflets because they may change your life."

"I'll read them," he promised sincerely.

Doug had been sentenced to only one weekend, and I never saw him again. I couldn't help wondering whether he read those tracts and responded to Christ.

One afternoon I came back to the barracks from my work assignment to find five of my Christian friends talking to about ten non-Christians. When they saw me come in, they called to me.

"Hey, Bruce, we need some help. We've been telling these guys about the return of Christ. Tell them what's gonna happen."

I shared with them the rapture of the church, the Antichrist's coming to rule the world, and the Lord's second coming. A few of these non-Christians later made decisions for Christ and became part of our group.

There were now many Christians in our barracks. When I didn't have to go to work on Sunday mornings, I would lead our group in a worship service. We would pray together and then I would share in the Word. All together, during the seven months I was serving weekends, about fifty men came to the Lord.

I was exhausted. No other prisoner was doing so many weekends; all others came and went before my time was up. When the last few weekends finally dragged by, I departed from Theo Lacy Jail with mixed emotions. The weary schedule was over, but in my heart I knew I would miss the fruitful jail ministry.

Chapter Sixteen
Mission Impossible

I had not been on a date since my conversion. Now that my weekends were free, I began to think about the possibility that God might bring a girl into my life.

I came across an excellent cassette tape entitled: "Finding God's Mate." It gave the qualities to look for in a spouse and told how God leads two people together.

The teacher explained that God prepares a perfect mate for each of us. Even though the two people don't know each other, God deals with both separately, preparing them for each other. "God does have a perfect mate for you," he said, "but many people settle for second best by getting too anxious. It is possible to marry another Christian and have a good marriage, but miss out on God's best by not waiting for his still small voice to speak.

"When a friend calls on the phone, you know who it is before he tells you, because you know the voice. If you spend enough time talking to God, you will know his voice. When he speaks and says, 'This is the one,' you'll know."

The tape spoke to my heart, and I became determined to wait for God's perfect mate. As I went to church, however, I would often find myself asking God, "Is this the one? Lord, she is really neat. Can that girl be your choice?" But of course, no voice out of the sky spoke to me.

For most of my life I dated attractive girls to impress other people. As a Christian I wanted to look at the inward person. I wanted a girl who was beautiful on the inside.

One evening I was invited to a Bible study and pot luck at Mansion Messiah, a Christian house run by the church. I arrived as the study was ending.

Moments after I entered the house, a pretty blonde came through the door. I'd known Debby Harper since my conversion, but had not been able to get close to her.

"Hi!" she said warmly. "I haven't seen you for a long time. What have you been doing?"

"I just finished my weekends in jail," I answered excitedly. Debby was with a girl friend, and the thought crossed my mind to get her alone to ask for a date. "Hey, I just bought a car. It's an Opel GT. Would you like to look at it?"

"Sure," she said, but all three of us walked outside. While we examined my car, Debby announced she was going to Santa Cruz on a missionary trip. She asked if I would like to go. I still had some commitments and couldn't break away, but I thanked her for asking. As she and her friend drove away, I reflected on how sweet she was.

Rick and I had decided to go to Utah to minister in Mormon country. I quit my job, and we went on our mission with several other Christian brothers.

When we arrived in Salt Lake City, the pastor of one of the local Baptist churches put us up in his house. He had provided a home for a number of non-Christian kids who had been living at a local park. His home and heart were wide open.

After we were situated, we prepared for our Sunday evening ministry. We decided it would be best to split up. Half our group went to our host's church to give the evening service. The rest of us went to the rescue mission located in downtown Salt Lake.

When we arrived at the mission, we discovered it was filled with teen-agers. These young travelers owned nothing but what they were wearing and had come for a free meal and a place to crash.

The mission director began the service and introduced us as a group of "Jesus people" from Southern California. Bob Cull, from our group, played a few Christian songs on his guitar. When Bob was done, I stood to give my testimony.

As I spoke, the Lord directed my attention towards several in the audience who seemed to be under conviction. I had expected no one to listen to my story, but most seemed hungry for the truth. When I had finished, Rick Nabors gave a message. He closed by asking if anyone wanted to become a Christian. About fifteen hands went up.

"If you want to accept Christ, we want to talk to you," Rick said. "We want to give you a free Bible and tell you more about the Christian life."

After the service eleven came up. Most had asked Christ into their lives during the service and were now wondering what they should do. Several of these new Christians were wanted by the police. Most of these men meant business. Some talked about turning themselves in. They were going to tell the judge how their lives had been changed. It was exciting to see God work in their hearts.

Outside the rescue mission, a half dozen street-walkers were soliciting the men on the other side of the street. Jimmy Kempner, one of our group, grabbed some Christian literature and ran over to the girls. When they realized he was a Christian and wanted to convert them, they backed up as if he had the plague.

172

We returned to the pastor's house singing and praising the Lord. The other group ministering at the Baptist church shared how God had blessed them too. Several people had rededicated their lives to Jesus as a result of their ministry.

Jimmy Kempner wal also a representative from Maranatha Music, one of the ministries of Calvary Chapel. He took several Maranatha albums to the local music station in Salt Lake. To our surprise, the radio station liked the music, and the next thing we knew, Christian music was being played on secular radio.

We had opportunities to share with all the young people in the house where we were staying. Because we didn't look like typical church kids, they couldn't understand why we loved the Lord so completely. Although the guys were antagonistic to our message, the girls asked sincere questions. It was obvious most of these kids had not really met Jesus Christ. Before we left, every girl became a born-again Christian.

One strange-looking man was staying at the house. He wore a coal-black beard that thoroughly covered his lower face. His matted and tangled hair came down over the rest of his face so only his nose and eyes showed, and he always wore dark sunglasses to conceal his eyes. He never washed and his clothes were filthy.

"Are you thinking what I'm thinking?" Rick asked when we first saw him.

"I sure am. There's an oppressive spirit in that guy."

"Let's pray for him," Rick proposed.

We began to pray quietly for this strange man on the other side of the room. He could not possibly hear us, but we could tell he was becoming irritable and paranoid as we prayed.

Later this strange fellow moved out, threatening to burn down the house with everyone in it. We were relieved when he moved back to the park.

We discovered a division had arisen among the Christians in Salt Lake. Many of the young people had left the organized church and were meeting at a self-styled "church in the park." The schism was causing real animosity between the two groups. We determined to help heal the wound and get the two groups together.

We planned an evening concert in our host's church. We put advertisements in the local paper, informed the minister of the church in the park, and passed out flyers to every Mormon we met.

On the night of the concert the church was packed. Several in our group gave musical presentations, then I was called up to give my testimony. When I finished, Jimmy Kempner preached on what it means to be born again. He explained it is like a caterpillar going through metamorphosis to become a butterfly. When he had finished his sermon, he gave an invitation.

A large number made first-time decisions, and an even greater number of Christians rededicated themselves to Christ. I was amazed by the number of older people who responded to the invitation.

After the concert, a striking dark-haired girl came up to me. I had noticed her while I was sitting on the platform, but had tried not to stare in her direction.

"Gee, Bruce the Lord has really given you a neat testimony. My name is Evie, and I'm working with Campus Crusade."

174

We talked for a while until I caught sight of an interesting fish symbol and cross she was wearing around her neck.

"That's really an attractively designed fish symbol," I observed.

"Believe it or not," she answered, "it was made here in Salt Lake by the Mormons."

"Really?"

"It was made at the copper mines here. I'm sure they don't know the fish is a symbol of Christianity, but a lot are made because so many Christians buy them. Here," she said, lifting the jewelry and chain over her head, "you can have it."

"Oh no, I don't want yours," I stammered. "I think it's nice, but I don't want you to give it to me."

"Bruce, I'd really like you to have it."

"Wow, Lord," I prayed silently to myself, "is this the one? She's really far out."

Evie was absolutely beautiful. Her long black hair fell below her waist and she was a slim five foot eight. She obviously liked me, and I was overjoyed the Lord had brought her into my life. Marriage bells were already ringing in my ear.

"Why don't you let me have your phone number? I'm gonna be coming up from Southern California a lot in the next couple of weeks; maybe we can fellowship together."

"That sounds neat, Bruce."

Evie gave me her number, and I was certain we would get together.

After the concert, we rejoiced that God had used us again. Many of the kids from the church in the park had come and the Lord had healed some of the wound between the two groups.

Rick and I decided to go witnessing the next night on State Boulevard where the kids in Salt Lake City hang out. On the street we could smell marijuana. Hundreds of cars were cruising up and down the boulevard. This Mormon town was much more wild than we had thought.

We carried our Bibles and a number of tracts and found many opportunities to talk to teen-agers on the strip. Most had been Mormons all their lives and loved God. Because of their religious background, we had no trouble getting them to talk about God. But as we shared the true gospel of Christ, we were continually asked one question. "By what authority are you preaching what you're preaching?" They felt we needed the approval of some higher power in the church.

"We've been led here by the Holy Spirit of God," I told them. "God ordains and anoints, and it is every Christian's right to preach the gospel. We're not here because we feel we have to be, but because God wants us here. We're speaking in the authority of Jesus Christ."

We shared how everyone must be born again. They claimed they already believed that, but their use of the terminology was not the same. They used the same words but they meant something completely different.

"Jesus Christ is all you need," we told them. "You can be complete in Christ; you don't need anyone else. Accept Christ into your heart and you have salvation; you don't need any special church."

"Gee, if we had that kind of religion, all you'd have is Jesus."

"Right! He's all you need."

They couldn't comprehend what we were saying. They had always had apostles, church elders, and church authority which had replaced a personal relationship with Jesus. Although most of the Mormon kids had too many religious hang-ups to respond to Christ, we did see a few decisions that night.

In the afternoon Rick and I went to several Mormon bookstores searching for material which would give us more ammunition to deal with the cult. In the Deseret Bookstore, owned by the Mormon church, we asked if they owned any old copies of the Book of Mormon or the Bible, because we were interested in doing a study on their religion.

They opened their vault to us and we were allowed to browse among some ancient volumes. We compared the modern day version of the Book of Mormon with those old copies and discovered many differences.

At the Mormon Temple we took pictures of everything we thought we could use in our ministry. While Rick was taking pictures, I suddenly realized we were being followed. Everywhere we went on temple grounds, men with walkie-talkies were watching us. After we left the grounds, they continued to tail us in cars.

We went into another Mormon bookstore later. It was a good-sized store and had the books and literature you would expect in any Christian bookstore. A salesgirl asked where we were from. We told her we were Christian ministers come from Southern California to share the gospel.

"Ministers? What church?" she questioned.

"We don't belong to any special denomination. We're members of the body of Christ. Don't you know every Christian is a minister of the gospel of Christ?''

She became more and more inquisitive as we talked. She had read many books and was quite knowledgeable, but was puzzled by the things we revealed about her church.

"We're not trying to cause confusion in your religious faith, but there's a big question before you. Jesus said you must worship God in spirit and truth. If you're not worshiping God in spirit and truth, then you're worshiping in error. If you're worshiping in error—you're not saved. Either you are born again and you're worshiping God the way he wants—or you're not. There's no middle ground.''

"What we've shown you proves you are not worshiping God in truth. God wants to have rich fellowship with you, but you're not having it because of the spirit of error within the Mormon church.''

She was deeply moved by our words, but we knew it would be difficult for her to make a decision right there because of her strong religious background. We knew she would investigate Christianity further after we left.

Through the week, one of my back teeth had been aching. Now the pain became unbearable. One of the girls in our house was working for a Christian dentist, and the next day found me in his chair.

"It's abscessed," he announced. "It's got to come out.''

"Oh no." I wasn't excited about the prospect of an extraction. "You *sure* it has to come out?''

"Well, you could have a root canal, but that's very costly.''

"Well . . . okay. If it has to go, it has to go.''

The dentist didn't give general anesthetic, instead he injected several novocaine shots into my mouth. As he tightened his pliers on the infected tooth, it became apparent the culprit was firmly rooted in my jaw.

"That molar is really in there. I'm afraid I'll have to chip away on it."

He began to pound on my tooth, and I began to feel like a rock pile. The shock of each blow caused me to break into a cold sweat. After several tense minutes of yanking, he finally extracted the molar.

I returned to our house with a numb head and a gaping hole in my mouth. I was scheduled to give my testimony at a Baptist church in Ogden. As the novocaine began to wear off, I took the drug the dentist had prescribed. I hadn't had any drugs for over a year, and right before I stood up to give my testimony, the pain-killer hit me.

A queasy feeling settled in my stomach as I stood up to testify. I felt foolish talking about a conversion from drugs with a light head. A piece of gauze in my mouth caused me to slur my words.

"Please be patient with me," I told the congregation. "I just had a tooth pulled this afternoon and they gave me a Darvon for pain. It's been a year since I've had any drugs and I feel a little queasy." I gave my testimony and Rick gave a message. There were three first-time decisions for Christ and a number of rededications.

I was invited to a church across town the next night while our group stayed at the Baptist church. The minister picked me up, and we had a great time sharing and praying in his car. Before we walked up on the platform, the pastor surprised me by saying,

"After I take the offering, the service will be yours. Give your testimony, preach a message, then give an altar call."

I gulped. I had never given a sermon, and didn't have one prepared. He was expecting me to do everything.

"Lord," I cried out silently as we walked on the platform, "you've got to take over. I don't know how to give a sermon. You've got to speak for me in a special way tonight."

Three or four hundred people were present by the time the pastor turned the service over to me. As I began to speak, God's Spirit took over and I felt power flowing through me. I could see the people in the audience who were on drugs or had been, and I began to talk to them. After I gave my testimony, I shared the things the Lord laid on my heart.

"You hear a lot about the Jesus people today and what's happening at Calvary Chapel. But it really isn't Calvary Chapel. It really isn't the Jesus movement either. It's Jesus, moving in the hearts of men and women. God has blessed some of us in having a direct part in what's going on, but Jesus isn't only moving in our area, he's moving all over the world. God wants a revival everywhere."

When the altar call was given at the conclusion of the service, six people came forward to receive Christ and a good number indicated they wanted to live for the Lord.

The next night I went on a date with Evie. We talked for hours. She shared all the things the Lord had done in her life and how she was involved with Campus Crusade. I shared what God had done in my life.

When Evie talked about the Lord, she revealed all kinds of things about herself that excited me. Evie was a dream. She was perfect. "She *has* to be the one," I reasoned. "She loves the Lord, and she's really pretty, and she even likes me. This must be it."

However, I remembered that tape on marriage and had to admit no still small voice was present. "Maybe God has already spoken to me, and I just didn't hear it," I suggested to myself. "She's just got to be the one. How can I let go of a girl as nice as Evie."

Chapter Seventeen
I'm in Love!

After our team returned to Orange County, I met a Christian girl who told me she was married to the Lord. She had given her love life to Christ and was committed to being single unless God clearly brought someone into her life.

The Lord told me I, too, had to become married to Jesus. I knew my affections had to be given over to God. "Okay, Lord," I prayed finally. "I give up. If you want me to get married, show me. I want my marriage to be miraculous; I don't want to make any mistakes. Give me peace, or I won't ever get married."

Rick and I and some other single brothers at the church began to call ourselves "bachelors to the rapture." Although Evie was still writing, I knew our relationship was over. I simply had no peace about it.

On a Friday night in August, after a Bible study at Calvary, I was talking to Mike Byrd and a few other Christian friends when out of the corner of my eye I saw Debby Harper making her way through the crowd. She looked beautiful. Her lovely blonde hair and pretty face captured my full attention. Debby seemed to glow as she walked up. Somehow, something was immediately different between us. She gave me an affectionate hug, and instantly the Lord spoke to me. A calm assurance flooded my soul: Debby Harper was to be my wife! The still small voice of the Lord was speaking, and she was *the one!*

Debby asked how the trip to Utah had gone, and I told her what the Lord had done. I asked how she was doing in school, and she told me. As we talked, everything and everyone dissolved and faded away.

Debby was so friendly. She loved the Lord so much. I wondered if I should ask for her phone number.

"Gee, Bruce, I never see you. It's been so long since I've seen you."

I had to ask for her number. She was being so sweet. If God wanted us together she would give it to me.

"Well, Debby . . . aaah . . . why don't you give me your phone number and we can talk about old times," I stammered, struggling for words.

"Sure, Bruce," she responded charmingly.

In a few minutes, we found a pencil and a piece of paper, and Debby wrote out her number for me. We continued to talk until everyone else had left the sanctuary.

182

When we finally parted company, I floated home. Our conversation had been so warm and friendly we had hugged four times. She was the one. I was in love and there was no doubt about it in my mind. I kept thanking the Lord.

When I decided to call Debby and ask for a date, I no longer had her number. I searched desperately for it, but to no avail. I wanted to call her in the worst way, but could not reach her. We returned to Utah shortly, and I wouldn't be able to see her for over a month.

Although I no longer had to do time in jail on my convictions, I was still required to serve out my probation on both the state and federal offenses.

On state probation I had to appear almost every month. They would contact me at different times and order me to come in on short notice to check my urine and blood for signs of drugs.

On one occasion I was on medication and suggested to the testing officer that it might show up.

"Yeah! I'll bet you were just taking medication! We've got you busted now!" When his report came back, however, nothing illegal was in my system.

At another time, I came in for my appointment bubbling over in the Holy Spirit. I was high on Christ. My probation officer took one look at me and ordered a series of tests. He couldn't understand why they, too, came out negatively.

My state probation officer always asked what I had been doing since he'd last seen me. So I shared how the Lord guided my life and gave me opportunities to share my faith with non-Christians. I witnessed to him indirectly, then asked him if he would like to come to church with me. He managed to decline graciously.

When I thought my witness was reaching him, I discovered they had assigned me to a new officer. This happened several times with both federal and state officers. It was as if no one knew what to do with me.

After an evening service at Calvary, I saw Debby walking out of the tent. She seemed in a hurry, but when she saw me, she smiled and waited.

After we had talked for a while, Debby said, "Bruce, I'm going to cut my hair shorter. What do you think?"

"Wow, don't cut your hair. Go home and read First Corinthians chapter 11. A woman's hair is her glory. Your hair is beautiful. You don't want to cut it off."

Another fellow came up and stood silently by Debby. I didn't know who he was, but the thought crossed my mind he might be her boyfriend.

Debby indicated she had to start for home, and I figured that would give me an opportunity to walk her to her car. But her friend started walking quietly on her other side. Although he said nothing, his presence made me feel uncomfortable. I didn't want to push myself at Debby if she already had a boyfriend, so I said good-bye and left them together.

I asked the Lord to work everything out. If Debby was going to be my wife, and the Lord was in the relationship, I wouldn't have to work at getting everything going—he would do that.

At the singles Bible study the next night, I was with a friend named Frank. After the fiasco of the night before, I was anxious to see and talk to Debby again. When the study was over, I discovered her sitting by herself, but was fearful of going over.

"Go ask her out," Frank ordered.

"No, no. I can't do that I don't know her that well."

"Then let's ask her to go to Coco's."

"I will. I will, just give me a minute," I stalled.

Frank could see I had lost my usual confidence, so he took matters into his own hands. He walked up to Debby and bluntly asked her to go to Coco's Restaurant with us—and she said "yes."

At Coco's, I found it difficult to look at Debby. Frank complimented her and said she should be a model. "She should be my wife," I told myself. "Man, I really love her."

When Debby had to leave, I walked her to her car while Frank waited in the restaurant. I opened the car door to let her in.

"Why didn't you call me?" she inquired innocently.

"I wanted to call you, but I lost your number. Can I have it again?" I asked nervously.

"Sure," she answered, reaching for her pen.

I wrote down her number, using my Bible to support the paper. Then I set my Bible in the backseat of her car while kneeling next to her window. We finished talking and Debby drove off. As I walked back into the restaurant, I realized my Bible was gone.

The next day I called Debby to see if she had my Bible. I was hoping she had it so I would have an excuse to go to her house.

"You left it in my car," she answered.

"Oh, that's good to hear. I was afraid maybe I'd lost it. I need it. Could you give me your address and how to get to your house?"

She gave me her address, and we talked warmly

185

for an hour. I began to wonder if I should ask her for a date. Rick was in the room with me. He was making wisecracks about my being in love, trying to make me laugh.

I wanted to invite her on a date badly, but if she said no, I knew I would die. I didn't know where we stood. "If it is God's will, she'll say yes," I reasoned.

"Would you like to go—" I began.

"Oh, yes, I'd love to!" she interrupted. "Where are we going?"

"To the Maranatha Concert Calvary's holding at Knott's Berry Farm?"

"Oh, that sounds far out. I sure would like to go, Bruce."

"Wow! Praise the Lord!" I said. "Just a second." I was too thrilled to stand still. I ran around the room before coming back to the phone. Rick was laughing at my childishness. When I hung up I told him what had happened.

"Wow, I can't believe this. She said 'yes' before she even found out where we're gonna go! I think she likes me!"

"Well, you finally got around to asking her out, didn't you?" Rick howled. "Man, I think you're gonna end up married. You won't make it single to the rapture."

"Hey," I blurted. "I want to see where she lives. I want to see her house."

I felt like a little kid. I had never felt like this toward any other girl. Rick went with me and we drove by her house. As we made a second pass, I decided to put a white rose on the windshield of her car.

The next night after the Bible study I saw Debby

again and asked her to go to Coco's. In the restaurant, the same guy who had stood by us when we talked after church, approached Debby and asked for a date. It was all I could do to look in the other direction as she politely refused his offer. After he left, we had a good time of fellowship.

That night I decided to put a pink rose on Debby's car. I left a note which read: "Debby, as you start this day, I pray this rose will brighten your walk with the Lord. Praise God."

I was apprehensive of being caught, so we parked down the street and I crept up behind her car. Using it to shield me from her house, I nervously placed the rose and note beneath the windshield wiper.

"If Debby catches me, she's going to think I'm a nut!" I shivered to myself. I slipped away quickly and quietly. I don't know what motivated me to leave roses, but my love was strong, and I couldn't express it any other way.

Next day I called Debby and asked her to go to church Sunday night. We talked for two hours on the telephone, but she didn't mention the roses. I asked how to get to her house again, to leave the impression I had never been there before. She hesitated for a moment, then gave directions again.

After church on Sunday, we went to Coco's once more, then I took Debby home. I could not return to leave a rose, so a small one was in my pocket. As we walked by her car, I reached over and faked taking the rose off her windshield.

"Look at this, Debby. Someone left a rose on your car."

"A rose on my car?" she questioned with a disbelieving smile. She held it up and tugged on my pocket, as if to say the rose was pocket size. "You know, Bruce, somebody's been leaving roses on the windshield of my car for the past few days."

"Really?" I replied nonchalantly.

"Yes," she continued. "I can't figure out who it is. It wouldn't by any chance be you, would it?"

"Me? You must be joking."

On Monday morning I discovered my schedule would cause me to miss going to her house again. "What am I gonna do?" I worried. "She attends a school in Santa Ana; if I can find that school, I can leave the roses on her car while it's in the parking lot."

Because I didn't know the name of the medical assistant school she was attending, I opened the telephone directory to the yellow pages. There was only one school in Santa Ana. "This must be the place."

I drove to the school and circled it several times, but couldn't spot her car anywhere. I began to wonder if it was the right school. Turning down a side street, I discovered her car, parked a block from the school. I pulled up quickly, and left a half dozen roses and another note.

> *I seek and pray for words, dear friend,*
> *My heart's true wish to send you.*
> *That you may know that far and near*
> *My loving thoughts attend you.*
> *I cannot find a truer word*
> *Nor better to address you,*
> *No song nor poem have I heard*
> *That's sweeter than God bless you.*
> *Praise the Lord.*

The next night I called Debby again. We talked for

two hours, and the subject of roses came up in our conversation.

"Bruce, I'm scared. Who knows where I go to school? I'm afraid someone is following me around."

I could tell she was getting frightened. Had I gone too far? "Debby, whoever is leaving those roses must really love you. You shouldn't be afraid." I felt funny admitting the rose-giver loved her. It seemed such an odd way to tell her my feelings, but I knew she needed comforting.

On the following weekend my brother was getting married in Las Vegas. It would be impossible to leave roses for two nights, so I asked Rick to take them over every night in my absence. I told Debby about the trip and sent her a postcard from Nevada to prove I really had left the area.

For some inexplicable reason, I could not keep silent about Debby at my brother's wedding. I predicted to everyone we were going to get married. Back in Orange County the following Monday, I went to church and announced to all my friends and acquaintances I was going to wed Debby Harper. It was a stupid thing to do, especially since we had not even gone out on a date, but I was so enamored I couldn't keep from sharing my feelings. The Lord had given me so much peace, I knew it would come to pass.

I called Debby and found she was ill. I bought a red rose, a get-well card with roses on it, and a box of candy, and went to see her. The moment she saw my presents, she knew I had given her all the roses.

"I didn't think it was going to get this complicated," I admitted. "I only planned to leave one rose, but it was so much fun I couldn't stop."

Even though she was sick, Debby prepared a delicious steak dinner. I contemplated how fantastic married life would be to this wonderful girl.

After dinner we sat on the couch and watched television. Debby placed her hand, tantalizingly, on the couch between us. It was a temptation. It was so graceful and seductive, I wanted to pick it up and squeeze it, but I stared passively at the television set. Each time I tried to move my hand towards it, cowardice overwhelmed me. "What if she rejects me?" I cringed. "If she spurns me, I'll die."

"Lord, give me boldness. Give me the power to take her hand. Lord, bind the power of Satan in Jesus' name!"

Finally I made my move. In one undramatic, ungraceful move, I picked up her hand and held it, and Debby responded by squeezing back!

My heart exploded with joy, but I sat stoically looking at the TV. I wanted to run around the room and shout, "Praise the Lord!" but I was afraid of destroying the mood. Never before had holding a girl's hand been of such significance to me.

We didn't do anything that night but hold hands and watch TV for two hours. Every few minutes she would squeeze my hand a little, then I would squeeze hers. Neither of us got much out of the TV program. Finally, I had to go home.

At my departure, I gave Debby a card which she was not to open until I had gone. The card said, "Love speaks always, but not always in words." Inside I wrote:

> *I thought perhaps you'd like to know*
> *What I've been up to lately.*

190

Something really wonderful,
It's raised my spirits greatly.
I've been visiting with Jesus,
And mostly about you,
Because I know He can cheer
As no one else can do.
I have the warmest feeling
As I leave the throne of grace,
For I've left you and your every need
In quite the safest place.
  Love in Christ,
     Bruce
  Praise ye the Lord.

On the phone the next day, I heard sobering news. "Bruce, the doctor told me I have pneumonia. He wanted to put me in the hospital, but he's not going to. But Bruce . . . I won't be able to go with you to that Maranatha Concert at Knott's Berry Farm. He doesn't want me out at night."

Depression swept my heart. The concert was only three days away. Was Debby really that sick, or was she using her illness as an excuse to break our date? "I must have blown it last night," I thought. "I never should have held her hand. I ruined the whole relationship in one night."

Debby must have sensed my gloominess. "Really, Bruce, please ask me out again. I want a rain check. I really want to go out with you."

Debby couldn't go out at night, but that wouldn't keep me from coming to see her. I came over almost every evening. Each time we saw each other, we read the Bible and prayed together.

One night after we had finished praying, we sat in front of the television set and held hands. I began to think how nice it would be to kiss her. "Wow," I thought, "if I try to kiss her, it may blow the whole relationship. But she knows how much I love her."

I turned towards Debby and caught her looking in my direction. She looked so kissable. In an instant, it happened. I had kissed her! Outside our window fireworks suddenly whistled and exploded from the high school football stadium across the street. We looked at each other and laughed. "Wow, that was some kiss," I cracked.

We kissed again, and this time, we heard bells and music in the distance. We laughed and hugged each other, praising the Lord.

On a Tuesday evening late in October, Debby was well enough to go to a Bible study at Calvary. We were so enchanted there must have been a glow around us. Everyone seemed to be staring at us. We were separated from others by a blissful bubble.

"Well, Bruce," Rick Nabors said. "You're sure on cloud nine. Where's your head at? You two are all spaced-out." Then he laughed. It was obvious what was happening to us.

After the study, we drove back to Debby's place and engaged in a heavy conversation. I asked Debby about her past boyfriends. She realized what I was driving at and shared her past.

"Before I was saved at fifteen," she said, "I had a lot of girl friends who had already had abortions. All my friends were going to bed with their boyfriends.

"I guess what kept me from going along with everyone else was my mother. She wasn't afraid to talk about sex. She made it sound great—for marriage. She explained that apart from marriage it would lose its meaning. There is nothing wrong with sex in itself, she told me. It's just like good rich soil, it's nice in the garden, but if you throw it on the living room carpet, it becomes a dirty mess.

"I also saw what happened to my girl friends when they gave in. They wouldn't see the guy again. I never got involved because I was thinking of my future husband. After I became a Christian, it was so much easier to keep from falling. I didn't have to depend on my own will power."

Debby's words moved me. I had been so promiscuous, and she had remained so pure. I didn't deserve such a precious girl.

"Debby," I confessed when she had finished talking, "I am in love with you."

She kissed me.

"Come on," I said nervously, "let's get on our knees and pray." We lifted up our relationship to the Lord and asked him to guide us. We wanted God's will in our lives.

After we prayed, I decided to share my feelings. I began to let down all the walls and barriers and exposed exactly how I felt.

"You're the kind of girl I could live with for the rest of my life. I know you have faults, but I can't see them. I'd really like you to be the mother of my kids."

Debby laughted, then blushed. She was innocent, yet mature. "You're so sweet," she responded shyly.

We both had so much peace. There was no confusion in our relationship. Neither of us seemed to have anything to do with what was happening. God's power was drawing us together.

Chapter Eighteen
The Witch

A week before Halloween, Debby was invited to speak at her old high school by one of her former instructors. The teacher was a Christian and wanted her to speak on her involvement with the occult.

I was astounded when Debby told me she had been a self-styled witch. She was too beautiful and innocent to be involved with demons; she just didn't look the type. I asked her how she became involved in witchcraft.

"It began when I was very young. As a little girl I was raised in an enormous house on a hilltop in San Jose. It was an old mansion with three stories and a cellar. It looked like an English castle. On the estate was a swimming pool, a small brick chapel which my father built for us kids, and a lodge where my father stored his many hunting trophies."

"Wow, you came from a rich family."

"That isn't half of what we had. My father owned a ranch with twenty horses, two beach houses, a couple of yachts. I always knew wealth and took it for granted everyone lived like us."

"What did your father do for a living?"

"He was a neurosurgeon. As a self-made man, he put himself through Harvard Medical School. He had seven heart attacks and knew he would die young, so he tried to make the most of life. He hunted big game all over the world and killed the largest Kodiac bear on record one year. He climbed some of the toughest mountains in the world, including the Matterhorn."

"He must have been quite a man. Was he a Christian?"

"No, he wasn't," she said sadly. "My mother came from a strong Christian family, though. Her father is a minister who wrote several Christian books and founded two Christian colleges. She started taking my brothers, sisters, and me to church, but my father didn't give her much help. For years she took us to different Protestant churches trying to find one that was excited about the Lord. She was really on her own, because none of us kids gave her much support either.

"Anyway, when I was very young that ancient house scared me to death. It was so monstrous, I got lost in it. I had a vivid imagination, and many strange things happened in that spooky place. I think it was possessed by demons. I would hear footsteps upstairs and knocking on the walls when no one was in the house.

"One night when I was three years old, I woke up to hear voices calling my name. Petrified, I woke up my sister Vicky who slept in the same room. She told me to go back to sleep, but how could I? I ran terrified through the house toward my parents' bedroom. To get to their room, I had to run through our massive living room. When I ran into it, several ghost-like people were sitting around the dining room table talking. They looked up at me. I dashed through the kitchen and past the breakfast nook, where I discovered a hand—with no body attached to it—just sitting on the leather seat. I darted into my parents' bedroom and jumped into their bed with them. This happened over and over until I was nine. I finally stayed in my parents' room."

"How did the rest of your family react to this?"

"They teased me. I'm the youngest of five kids, and my two older brothers and two sisters made up stories and played practical jokes on me. Everyone, including my father, enjoyed making me cower at the thought there were ghouls in the house. This was back when no one believed in demons. Today people don't doubt like they did when I was a girl.

"When I was nine, we moved to another house in the Santa Cruz area. I made friends quickly and soon began to go to slumber parties. At the first one I went to, someone brought a Ouija board. I'd never heard or seen a Ouija board before and was fascinated. The fantasy world excited me, and I longed to know more about the supernatural.

"The next day I bought myself a Ouija board at the local toy store. My mother was so upset she told my father about it. He told her not to worry because it was just a game.

"I started inviting girls to my house for slumber parties, and we always fooled around with the board half the night. Things always happened. We got results, and I began to feel I was catching on well to how the board worked. I remember thinking the other girls didn't know as much as I did.

"In fifth grade, I started to think about leading my own seances. I had seen them on television and began to buy any book which dealt with the subject. Back then, very few books were available, but I found works on ESP, telepathy, and astrology, and also bought tarot cards. I even made a voodoo doll of an ex-boyfriend, and began to stick pins in it. My mother found it and burned the doll in the fireplace. She was very disturbed with me and destroyed my Ouija board as well.

"Even without the board, I began to have my own seances. We had them in our guest room where I always had my slumber parties. I convinced my

196

friends to sit around a table upon which we placed a lighted candle. I asked Satan to come into our presence and we could actually tell a spirit was in the room. A distinctly cold chill appeared and the candle flame moved like a breeze was blowing.

"My girl friends were terrified by what we were doing, but I felt tremendous power and I wanted to turn them on to it. As we sat around the table, we asked Satan questions. Each night we changed the sign for his answers. One knock was 'no,' and two knocks was 'yes.' To keep anyone from knocking on the table, we held hands and touched feet. When we started getting knocks on the wall and table, most of my friends became so petrified they wanted to quit. It was all I could do to keep everyone at it.

"Late one night I asked Satan to get Marilyn Monroe's spirit. This particular night, the sign the spirit had come into our presence was to be a cat's meow.

"A loud screech outside caused us to freeze. We knew a spirit was in the room. I told the spirit we wanted proof she was with us by messing up the bathroom and giving a sign when she was done. There was only one door to the rest room, and only one window, two stories above ground. It was straightened before we made the request.

"Another screech outside caused us to huddle closely together. Carefully we opened the door and discovered the room was totally messed up. Two stockings which had been hanging up were now on the floor. The toilet seat which had been up, was now down. The rug was pushed up against the wall and the cupboards had all been opened. There was absolutely no way any of us could have messed up that bathroom.

"The girl standing behind me beheld an image of

197

blonde hair and a pretty face in the mirror. I saw it too. Another girl glimpsed what appeared to be a black slip. We had interrupted the spirit while she was still in the bathroom. In terror we pushed the door closed and huddled in the center of the room as one clinging mass. The bathroom door opened by itself, there was a rush of wind across the room, then the locked door leading into the rest of the house opened and slammed. Something had literally moved through our room. I'm not kidding, Bruce, it really happened."

"Oh, I believe you. I've had just enough experience with demon-possessed people to believe Satan and his demons are real! What happened after that?"

"Well, most of my girl friends were so frightened they never wanted to try anything like that again. But the experience convinced me there was a definite spirit-realm, and something inside attracted me to it. When my girlfriends would no longer come to my seances, I started talking to spirits alone in my room. I prayed to Satan and asked him for powers."

"Didn't you know it was wrong to pray to Satan, Debby?"

"I was only thirteen, but my involvement with the occult was so heavy I began to do many things I never normally would have done.

"One night, while I was in bed, an old woman's voice called me to come outside to her. It really scared me and I wondered if it had just been my imagination. Then I heard her again. I was so frightened, I pulled the covers over my head and waited for her to leave. Nothing more happened that night.

"A couple of nights later the same old-sounding

voice called me out again. I was frightened and wanted to hide, but I began to question my fear. If I wanted supernatural power, I would have to get involved with spirits. Finally I told the spirit I would go with her.

"I crawled out my window with my dog Tiger. I walked to some eucalyptus trees. I talked to the trees and the wind and they talked back to me. As the leaves rustled, I could hear words. Whenever I sensed a spirit was present I would observe my dog. He could sense such things, and would look around as though someone was standing there. This time we both felt the presence of spirits.

"With experiences like this, I became more enchanted with the supernatural. I never told anyone what I was doing, but my mother discovered I was going out at night when she found my screen latch unhooked. By now mother was extremely worried and was constantly praying for me.

"A woman down the street owned all kinds of cats; there was something about cats that attracted me. I felt in tune with their spirits.

"One day a large black cat came out in the middle of the street and for some unexplainable reason I started talking to the animal in another language. It was like some kind of 'tongue.' The cat understood me and I knew, somehow, there was a witch's spirit in it. I later learned this is often how demons reveal themselves. When I stopped talking, the cat vanished! I feel like an idiot telling you this Bruce, but that cat actually vanished right in front of my eyes.

"Although I went to church every week and believed in God, I was being swept off my feet by an intense desire to be involved more deeply in the supernatural world. I was reading *The Forbidden Knowledge of Good and Evil*, which I was later told was the satanic bible.

"My whole family expected my father to die of a sudden heart attack. Every night I asked God if my dad would be alive the next morning. I always seemed to know he would be okay.

"One evening I felt no answer. I received nothing. It was as if my father was going to die before morning. I began to cry and fled to my sister's room. Vicky was weeping too, but when I asked what was wrong, she didn't know. I went back to bed and sobbed myself to sleep.

"At eleven o'clock, my mother woke me and said dad had had another heart attack and had died. I knew what she said was true.

"My father had never understood how deeply I had gone into the spirit world. To him, I was always his innocent little baby who could do no wrong. I really looked up to my father. He was the major reason I hadn't gotten involved with drugs. He said the brains of people who had used LSD looked like Swiss cheese. I don't know if he told the truth, but it scared me. Once he died there were no more pep talks, and I began to wonder if I was missing some of the good things in life.

"As an eighth grader, I started taking marijuana and quickly grew to like it. I tried whites and from there went to LSD. I really liked LSD and took it all the time. I smoked pot before school, during school, and after school. After getting home, I would drop mescaline or acid, get drunk, then go to bed."

"Did your family have any idea you were taking drugs?"

"My mother kept finding my drugs, but I always told her they weren't mine. I don't think she could imagine me taking drugs.

"I became very introverted and withdrawn. I didn't see my family too much while on drugs, but when I did, there was almost always a fight.

"One afternoon I exploded into a rage and screamed my hatred for everyone in the family. I ran into my room, slammed the door, and latched both locks.

"My brother Rick was so upset he charged after me. He had a brown belt in karate, and his fist came smashing through my door, shattering a mirror and sending it crashing on the floor. His other fist punctured the door and he reached around to unlatch the two locks. Rick crashed into my room, sending the whole door slamming to the ground. I fled to my bed screaming hysterically at the top of my lungs.

" 'Get out of here! I hate you! Look what you've done! You tried to kill me with that mirror! You're so violent! You're not my father and I don't have to listen to you!'

"Rick just stood there. He couldn't believe my bitterness; we had always been so close. Mother ran into the room crying; then Rick broke down and wept too. He knelt beside my bed, grabbed my hands and began sobbing a prayer out loud. 'Lord, I lift Debby up to you. I pray you will come back into this family and change the commotion we're having. Lord, please change Debby's life.'

"I listened to his prayer, but when he was done I breathed with a special bitterness, 'I hate you! Leave me alone and get out here. Who do you think you are anyway?'

" ' Debby,' Rick told me, 'I love you.' He was still crying and obviously heartbroken.

"But I continued to shriek hatred. 'That does nothing to me. Get out of here! Get out of my life!' I screeched. I think that was the lowest point in my life. I had grown so hard.

"After that experience, positive things started happening. My grandparents gave me a modern translation of the New Testament for Christmas, and although I was still getting loaded, I began to read it often. Jesus began to fascinate me.

"The more I read the Bible, the more my life was affected. I stopped taking psychedelic drugs, but continued smoking marijuana. I was doing my best to be a Christian. I began to tell my friends they should trust Jesus to take care of their problems, but I didn't practice what I preached.

"I bought a record of a popular Christian singing group and the music began to speak to me. The words of almost all of the songs came from Scripture, and they pierced my heart.

"My mother suddenly felt God wanted our family in Newport Beach. She felt he wanted to get me out of Santa Cruz and away from my drug-taking friends. She put our house up for sale and it sold the same day.

"When we arrived in Orange County I enrolled at Corona Del Mar High School and quickly met a group of kids who got loaded. I went to several parties, but it bothered me that everyone needed to be high. I wondered if I, too, needed drugs to be happy, and for the first time I could see what was happening to my life. I had to smoke a joint to feel normal. My memory and grades had literally gone to pot.

"Over summer vacation I didn't associate with any of my new friends. The more I read the Bible, the more God spoke to me. One day I looked at a joint in my hand and asked why I needed it. A Scripture came to mind: 'Whatever you give unto me I will give you back a hundredfold.' Did that mean if I gave up marijuana God would give me more in return?

"I thought of what one of my Sunday school teachers had shared. 'Whenever you hurt someone, you hurt Jesus because he feels every sorrow and pain.' At this point in my life, I couldn't stand my mother, but I loved Jesus. I didn't want to treat her badly anymore because Christ loved her and felt the pain I was inflicting.

"I knew it was time to make a decision. Every time Billy Graham was on television, I had made a decision for Christ, but nothing ever happened, because I wasn't willing to give up my old life.

"As I sat thinking, I decided to sincerely let Jesus have control of my life. I prayed to him. I didn't just ask him to come into my heart, I gave my heart to him. This time I asked him to straighten out my messed up heart and forgive my sins.

"I remember telling the Lord, 'If you will give me back a hundred-fold like you say, I'll give up my pot for one week; but if you don't come through, I'll go back to it.' That night I cried myself to sleep, but the next morning I possessed a tremendous feeling of joy. I had peace with God and felt a strong desire to love all those around me.

"I told Rick and my mother what had happened, but they were skeptical. It must have been difficult for them to believe a real change had taken place, because I lied so often.

"I took all my drugs and flushed them down the

toilet. I was no longer sacrificing them for God, I didn't want them anymore. Jesus had given me more than drugs could ever give, and I knew it.

"Picking up my Bible, I turned to that passage which says, 'They that call upon the Lord shall be saved.' For the first time that verse made sense. I had been blind and was finally seeing what the Bible was talking about. It spoke as it had never spoken before.

"Back at school I didn't want to associate with the same kids. I began praying for a Christian friend. I was wearing a cross one day and a girl asked if I was a Christian. She invited me to Calvary Chapel, and we went that night.

"There were so many young people and adults loving each other it made me want to cry. God had thoroughly answered my prayers. I had always wanted something supernatural and this was it. The Holy Spirit was obviously in the church. Everything was real and true, and so much better than anything Satan could have offered.

"It took a year for me to prove myself to my family. They thought I was using Calvary as a cover to do what I wanted. Finally they realized God had really reached my heart and both Rick and my mom began to come to church with me. Rick got reborn and we got baptized together. Eventually everyone in my family came to know the Lord, and Rick and I had the privilege of watching them all get baptized."

A couple of days later, Debby gave her testimony at the high school Bible study and related most of what she had shared with me. She told the young people how easy it is to get involved in Satanism by dabbling with Ouija boards and other forms of the occult.

Chapter Nineteen
Gettin' Hooked

On Halloween night, Debby and I went out to dinner. We ate at a Mexican restaurant, then drove south to Laguna Beach. The city was swarming with merrymakers attired in bizarre costumes. We cruised up and down Pacific Coast Highway and observed the revelers.

"Bruce, what's on your mind?" Debby inquired sweetly.

"Oh, nothing," I fibbed.

I couldn't look her way. I was afraid she could read my mind. I had almost decided to ask Debby to marry me and was searching for words.

Leaving the city we traveled to a quaint spot called The Top of the World, in the Laguna hills. We steered up the winding road and passed through some clouds. Once on the top, we beheld a gorgeous panorama. Our eyes scanned the horizon up the coast towards Newport Beach. The ocean reflected the city lights and created a dazzling scene.

"Bruce, I know something's on your mind. Why don't you talk about it?"

"No, no, it's nothing," I apologized again.

As we started back towards Laguna, Debby persisted in her questioning. "Come on, Bruce, talk about it. I can tell something is on your mind."

"Well," I answered finally, "I was trying to figure out how to ask you to marry me."

She looked at me for a moment, then said, "What?"

"Debby, will you marry me?" I asked boldly.

There was silence in the front seat. Debby didn't

say anything. I began to think I had blown it again when she snuggled up to me.

"You know what, Bruce?"

"What?"

"I've been talking to God about our relationship lately, and asking him to confirm it. Every time I've opened my Bible, I've turned to passages that deal with marriage." She paused for a few moments. "Bruce, let's seek the Lord and make certain it's his will."

Debby had not said "yes," but she certainly had not said "no." The fact that she had been seeking the Lord about marrying me was exciting. As far as I was concerned, God had spoken.

Two days later, Debby came to my apartment, and we talked about marriage. We both agreed a Christian marriage had to be a ministry. Two have to be able to serve Christ better together than apart. The ceremony scared us both, and we discussed the possibility of eloping. We then talked about the number of kids we would have—at least four— and decided we would wed in six months.

"Bruce, I want to take care of you, feed you, love you, and spoil you."

"Praise the Lord," I sighed.

Later in the week, at a Bible study, I calmly announced our engagement to a friend. Debby was surprised by my sudden proclamation, but after the study she made an announcement of her own.

We walked up to pastor Chuck Smith and Debby gave him a hug. Chuck had spent many hours counseling her and was like a second father.

"Chuck, Bruce and I feel the Lord is bringing us together for marriage."

"Praise the Lord!" Chuck responded. A big smile swept his face and he put his arms around us both.

206

That week I told my state probation officer of my plans for marriage. "Now wait a minute," he cautioned. "You have to have permission from the state to get married."

"You're kidding."

"No, I'm not. You need permission from us. We want to make sure you're emotionally and psychologically mature enough to handle marriage. You've been through a lot. If you get in over your head, you may go back to dealing and get in trouble. We can't let that happen. We want to make certain it's not too much for you."

"I want to get married," I responded in exasperation. "I'm ready. I wouldn't be getting married if I wasn't. I'll never go back on drugs. I've never been so emotionally and psychologically mature as I am right now. If we have financial problems, my wife can always work. We'll make it."

"Why don't you bring in your fiancée, and we'll talk about this further."

It was clear the probation officer didn't understand what had happened in my life. He felt there was a possibility I might go back to drugs. He did not know how thoroughly I had been transformed by Christ.

Debby came in later. The officer softened as he realized she was not an infatuated kid. Debby was a mature young lady, and he realized we both knew what we were doing.

As we talked, the probation officer opened up and related problems he was having with his own kids. We almost started counseling him. Most probation officers have few lasting answers for juvenile problems. Kids don't respond to the average approach. This probation officer realized, as many others had, that a transformation brought on by a personal relationship with Christ is one of the few real answers to social problems.

Before Debby and I left, the officer informed me he would recommend I be taken off state probation two years early. Within a matter of weeks, this happened.

A few days later my father entered the hospital with severe stomach pain. Dad had seemed so healthy at my brother's wedding. The doctor diagnosed Dad's problem as cancer and gave him only one chance in ten of pulling through. The Scripture passage came to mind which says, "What is your life, it is but a vapor that appears for a little while, then vanishes away."

Dad had not been told he had cancer, but he seemed to know. As we talked in his hospital room, his eyes communicated this might be the last time we saw each other. Dad had not met Debby, and I began to worry he might never see her. With all the sorrow I had caused him, I hated to think he might miss seeing our wedding.

At the first opportunity, I took Debby to the hospital. They had Dad on drugs, and his reasoning was affected.

"Dad, I'd like you to meet Debby, the girl I'm gonna marry."

Dad took Debby's hand and said, "You're beautiful, Debby. Bruce, you don't deserve such a sweet young lady."

"Well, Mr. Danzara, I don't deserve a handsome young man like Bruce," Debby responded, and we all laughed briefly.

Later when Dad and I were alone, he told me, "I

don't believe it, Bruce. It is a miracle you're marrying Debby. She's darling. I got very good vibrations from her. She's the right girl for you, Bruce. She'll make you an excellent wife.''

"I know, Dad. She's the Lord's choice."

My father's illness caused me to trust God more fully. There was absolutely nothing I could do but pray. I poured myself out to God. My prayers were deeper than they had been for a long time. The Lord was putting me through his discipline.

Dad went into surgery three days later. At 9 A.M., Mom, my sister, and I waited and prayed in the hospital lobby. By 3:00 in the afternoon, I had lost almost all hope my father would make it. I wondered how I could comfort my mother.

The doctor appeared with a sober, tired face. His expression immediately confirmed my worst fears, but I was surprised by his words.

"Mrs. Danzara, it was a long operation, but everything's fine. We removed a tumor the size of a grapefruit, but it was a clean removal and it doesn't seem to have spread anywhere else. We had to remove one of his kidneys and his spleen. He's in intensive care now, but he should pull through all right."

"Praise God!" we all breathed together.

"Doctor, can Dad live all right without his kidney and spleen?"

"He has another kidney of course, so he can get by nicely without one. His body will have to adjust to the loss of his spleen, but he can survive quite well without it."

We were able to visit intensive care the next morning. I didn't expect what we saw. A monitor screen stood beside his bed registering each heartbeat. Tubes were running in and out of his body, and he was extremely pale. He didn't look good. While I was in the room, he woke, but was too drugged to respond.

After a few days, Dad was out of intensive care and in a regular hospital bed. They said he would be released in two weeks, and we were all unusually thankful.

Engagement gave my life a whole new perspective. No longer could I live footloose. For six months I had lived on savings from the uniform supply job; now only $30 was left in my bank account, and I had to find a job.

After looking for a long time, I finally found work in a steel factory. It was a dangerous place, and the pay wasn't what I had hoped for, but it was a job. The work was extremely physical and I wore out a pair of work pants and heavy duty gloves every two or three days.

While I was driving home one night, my car engine started ticking. The noise changed to a loud knocking as I pulled over. I knew a major repair job was necessary, and I didn't have the money. I parked in a gas station and called a friend for a ride home. Things seemed to be going badly, but I continued to rejoice in the Lord. Life is always exciting when you realize you are in God's hands.

Debby began to take me to and from work. It was hard on her, because she was still attending school full-time, but we had no alternative.

After only two weeks at the steel factory, I knew it was time to quit; I had no peace about the job.

Without knowing the future, I severed employment and began to look for another job.

I received a call from an old friend who wanted me to work for him. He said it would pay $150 a week take-home, but would go up from there. He ran an engineering firm and said I would be spraying the roofs of industrial buildings with a substance designed to protect them from the weather. He wanted me to start immediately. I decided to take the position.

After Christmas, I was in Debby's living room, and noticed her diary sitting on the coffee table. I picked it up as she walked into the room.

"Oh, you don't want to read that," she said sweetly.

"Why not?" I teased. "Is there something you don't want me to see?"

"No, you can read it if you want."

We began to leaf through her diary together. I wanted to see what Debby had been thinking when we started dating. I flipped through page after page which talked of an old boyfriend. Then on August 18, we came to an entry where Debby had written she was in love with me. After that entry, the diary began to talk about her ex-boyfriend again.

"What happened on the 18th?"

"That was the Friday night at Calvary when you asked me for my phone number, remember?"

"Yeah! That was the night the Lord revealed to me you were going to be my wife. Did the Lord talk to you that night too?"

"He sure did. I had just broken up with a boyfriend and didn't want anything to do with guys. But when I saw you, there was a glow around you. No foolin'. Looking at you made me wonder what I had been doing. The boys I dated seldom wanted to share Christ. I suddenly realized you had the spiritual qualities I wanted in a husband.

"You know," Debby continued, "before I went to church that night, a feeling came over me that I would see my future husband. As I think back, I told my mother my husband was already my friend, I just didn't know who he was yet. When I saw you, I knew. It was like sticking my finger into a light socket."

"Did you want me to ask for your phone number?"

"Did I?! I kept praying you'd ask. I was so friendly to you! I wanted you to ask in the worst way."

"Wow," I remarked, "it's neat to know the Lord spoke to you the night he spoke to me. That gives even more assurance our marriage is God's will."

As Debby and I continued to date, we found ourselves being tempted physically. The Bible says to flee youthful lusts; we decided to read the Word of God on our dates.

A verse in Galatians was especially powerful in keeping me from temptation. It said, "I say then, if you walk in the Spirit you shall not fulfill the lusts of the flesh." I didn't have to try to be good if I was walking in the Spirit. So every time temptation knocked, I made certain I was walking in the Spirit. In this way, we were able to have victory in our dating.

We decided on a small garden wedding in the backyard of Debby's house. Our main purpose in the ceremony was to testify to our non-Christian friends. They would not come to church, but they would come to our wedding. We planned to center everything around the Lord. March 15 was to be the date.

In February, Debby and I went shopping with her mother and stepfather and selected wedding invitations, napkins, plates, and flowers. We also picked out rings, which we custom-designed with Christ-centered symbolism.

Debby graduated from medical-assistant school a week before we were scheduled to wed. We still had not decided if I should rent a tuxedo or buy a good dress suit. At the last minute we decided to buy a suit. The suit had to be altered and we spent the rest of the week looking for shoes and a shirt to go with it.

Rick Nabors, my best man, teased me about having a bachelor party. I didn't really want one, but he talked me into it. At the party, Rick told of a groom he knew who had his legs shaved when he went to sleep after his bachelor's party. He said if I went to sleep they would shave my legs. I stayed up all night and Rick didn't come through on his threat.

At six o'clock the next afternoon our wedding began. Bob Cull played the piano and sang. His music clearly presented Jesus Christ.

Before our wedding I had counted the hours. Now I counted the minutes and was extremely nervous. No sleep the night before certainly didn't help my composure. Rick laughed at my jitters.

Debby was in one part of the house and I was in another so we wouldn't see each other until the ceremony. Rick and I walked to the side of the house. We were standing next to a palm tree growing beside the pool.

Chuck Smith appeared through the foliage and joined us. He could see I was almost in shock. He gave me one of those warm smiles he's famous for.

"Praise the Lord," he beamed.

"This is heavy, Chuck. This is really heavy."

The three of us walked to the patio where the ceremony was to be performed. Everything was in slow motion. Debby was escorted out by her brother Rick. She was absolutely beautiful in her white flowing wedding dress. Her maid of honor was her sister Bunny. I took Debby's arm and faced Chuck.

People had fumbled through their vows at many of the weddings I had attended, and I feared doing the same thing. A cotton ball was in my throat.

"Oh, Lord, speak through me today!" I prayed. "Give me the strength to make it!"

Chuck began to quote the words of the Apostle Paul: "Husbands, love your wives as Christ loved the church." It would be impossible to love Debby that much, and the thought overwhelmed me with fear. But then God comforted with his peace. It was as if the Lord was saying, "Look, Bruce, I have brought you this far—I'll stay with you through your marriage. I'll give you the love necessary to make Debby happy. Just trust in me."

The ceremony wasn't long, but it seemed like a marathon to me. Debby's grandfather gave us communion at the beginning of the service. Even though we had pillows to kneel on, I developed a cramp in my leg and fidgeted through that part of the service.

Chuck led us through the vows and Debby struggled to place the ring on my finger. She pushed several times before it slipped on. My finger must have swollen. Debby's ring went on easily.

Chuck looked at us through a big smile and said, "I now pronounce you man and wife. What God has joined together, let no man break asunder."

I turned and kissed my new wife. Everyone rushed up to congratulate us. We walked into the house where Debby's parents had catered a buffet dinner which included beef stroganoff, rolls, punch, and a large wedding cake.

All our Christian friends and relatives were sharing Christ with all our non-Christian acquaintances. Debby's mother was sharing with Brad, the friend who had first turned me on to marijuana. One person became a Christian as a result of that reception.

We left the house at ten thirty that evening. As we walked towards Debby's car, everyone threw "puffed rice" at us. Cans were hooked on the back of the car and someone wrote "Just Married" with shaving cream on the vehicle's side. Oil had been smeared on our front windshield. My dad and Debby's stepfather cleaned it off as best they could, but as we drove down the coast, it began to rain, and the oil smeared even further by our windshield wipers. It was difficult to see, but we were both in such a state of euphoria it was difficult to notice either the window or the weather.

We arrived in Leucadia, just north of San Diego, after midnight. I had rented a beautiful beach house constructed on the edge of a cliff overlooking the Pacific. By the time we arrived, the rain had abated, but fog had moved in.

I carried Debby over the threshold, then brought in our luggage. We began to prepare for bed. I went into the bathroom and it dawned on me I was scared. Butterflies were flying in my stomach. After I had been in the bathroom for some time, Debby called to me.

"Bruce, is anything wrong? What's taking you so long?"

"I'm coming," I said. "I'll be out in a minute." But I hadn't even taken off my shoes.

After so many years in the world, I couldn't believe God had completely made me over. I had had so much experience, but now I was a new person all over again. I thanked God that "the blood of Jesus Christ, his Son, cleanses us from all sin." Praise the Lord!

Chapter Twenty
You Only Live Twice

We returned to our apartment and set up housekeeping. Although I was working full-time I still found many opportunities to share my faith. One night I pulled into a small market to buy a newspaper and looked up into a familiar face.

"Bruce, I didn't recognize you with short hair. Could you give me a ride?"

"Oh hi, Denise. Where do you want to go?"

Denise had known me in the world. We had been at many of the same pot parties. I had witnessed to her after my conversion, but it had been a year and a half since we had seen each other. I gave her a lift, and we talked about old times.

"You know," she said soberly, "I held Sandy's death against you for over a year. I blamed you for her death and hated God for letting it happen."

"I didn't know you knew Sandy."

"She was one of my best friends and we spent a lot of time together. When you said you were a Christian, I wouldn't believe it because of what you did. Do you still believe in God? I expected you to be back into drugs by now."

"I love the Lord more now than I did a year and a half ago. My relationship with the Lord grows deeper all the time."

Tears formed in her eyes. "I need God. I need him in my life, or I won't be able to make it." She started to get out of my car.

"Denise, my wife and I would love to have you over for dinner some night. Maybe we can all go to church together."

"Please call me, Bruce. I really want to go to church with you." She quickly ran off.

The next day I phoned Denise at her home in Dana Point and invited her to a Saturday night concert. During that service, both Debby and I prayed she would respond at the invitation, but she made no outward decision.

When we drove her home that night, we became hopelessly lost, but getting lost was God's will. It gave us another hour to share Christ.

Finally, Denise said, "I want to tell you something. While you were talking, I felt the Lord speak to me and I asked Jesus into my heart."

"Praise the Lord!" Debby responded.

No sooner had she said those words than we came out on Pacific Coast Highway. In a matter of minutes we arrived at her front door. Before she left the car, I gave her a *Jesus Lives* newspaper produced by Calvary.

The next day she called. "I want thousands of those papers. Everybody at work was reading the one you gave me. You know why it took me so long to trust Jesus, Bruce? I've known so many people who made a decision for Christ but later gave it up, that I wanted to make sure I'd stick with it."

My employer was having hard times and dropped my pay. My pay fell from $150 to $60 a week and sometimes I was not paid at all. A Christian friend suggested I apply at the construction company where he worked. Although I witnessed to a foreman and the company vice-president for three hours, they hired me as an apprentice carpenter.

After a month on the job, I again had no peace. It was the same feeling the Lord had given at the steel factory. "What's wrong, Lord? I'm making good money, and the job is enjoyable. I thought this job would be it. What's wrong?"

Because I presented my body and mind to the Lord each day as a living sacrifice, I knew he was in control. The Lord was saying I would not be at this job long.

Pastor Chuck spoke on knowing God's will for your life one night. He said people often spend their lives working at jobs they don't enjoy. "If you want to know what God wants you to do, do what you enjoy doing most. God gives his peace at the employment he wants you to have."

Everywhere I went, my ministry to souls was the most important part of my life. At any job, the main thing on my mind was to talk about the Lord. Whenever I preached or led a Bible study, I possessed an overwhelming peace.

That night God spoke to me about my future. From that moment I knew he wanted me in the ministry. But God also made it clear if I was going to become a minister, I would have to prepare myself. I would have to go back to school.

I could graduate from a Bible college in two years, and on Chuck's recommendation, I applied at Southern California College, a Christian school near

Calvary. They accepted me, and I quit my job to attend college full-time.

Bible college was different from my previous college experience. The major textbook was the Bible, and although we had many other books, classes were like in-depth Bible studies. SCC was much harder than the secular college I had attended. Almost every class required a term paper, and I had never done one before.

All my life I had run from responsibility, but the Lord had put me into a situation in which I would have to study hard to graduate. I needed the discipline this Christian college offered.

Our money began to get low again, but we continued to trust the Lord. We knew he would take care of our needs, and provide for our future as well. Debby began looking for a job as a medical assistant to help us make ends meet. After looking for a long while, she was finally able to land a good position.

Pastor Chuck came up to me one Sunday morning and said, "Bruce, how would you like to teach some Bible studies?"

"Praise the Lord! I'd love to."

For months I had been thinking about getting involved in the ministry at Calvary but felt it would be wrong for me to ask. If God wanted me in the ministry, he would open a door and make it clear. God was now opening that door.

I was given Rancho High School in Garden Grove, my alma mater. I had sold drugs on that campus, and it was exciting to return with a new message. I began to teach a weekly Bible study on campus.

I finished the fall term with an A-minus average. In junior college, I had cheated my way to a C average. For the spring semester I dropped some units and picked up a part-time job. By the Lord's grace, we continued to make it financially.

Before too long, I was leading four high school Bible studies and three home fellowships for the church. Over the next few months I helped plan a number of youth activities at Calvary. Twice I taught at Calvary's new conference grounds in the mountains. The more ministry I participated in, the more certain I became the Lord wanted me in his work.

I was put on part-time staff and my duties increased. I began to teach the Tuesday night Bible study for high school students and was given my first counseling responsibilities.

I had counseled many people as God provided opportunities. Now that I was on staff I began to look forward to my first counseling appointment.

He was a man in his forties who had glassy-looking eyes. He was shaking all over. "Wow," I thought, "this man looks like he's on the verge of a nervous breakdown." When he began to pour out his problems, my fears were confirmed.

"About a week ago," he began, almost in a daze, "I lost my job. Two days ago, my wife left me. Last night my house burned to the ground—everything I've worked for for twenty years is gone—and I didn't have any insurance. Because we were out in the cold last night, my little girl caught pneumonia. I just left her at the hospital. Everything I've ever worked for is gone . . . all I have left is the clothes on my back."

"Oh, Lord," I prayed silently, "what am I going to tell him? If I say 'all things work together for good,' he'll want to hit me in the mouth."

I could almost hear the Lord say, "Bruce, tell him I love him and show him that verse."

I felt like arguing with the Lord. To say "God loves you" was too simple. But somehow, as I said those very words, I realized it was exactly what he needed to hear. He needed to know that God had allowed this to happen so that he would come back to him.

He admitted being a backslider, and said he would not have sought counsel if his life had not fallen apart. I shared several Bible verses with him and we prayed before he left.

Later he came back to tell me that his wife had returned, his child was now well, and he had gotten a good job. Not as wealthy as before, he now realized he had been trusting in things. Before, his happiness depended on life's circumstances, now he was looking to Christ for fulfillment. He was certain God had purged his life to bring him back into fellowship.

On another occasion, when I was the only minister in the office, the secretary informed me that a couple was coming in who had just lost their three-year-old baby boy.

"Oh, Lord!" I prayed. "What am I going to say? How can I possibly comfort them?"

When the couple arrived, they were holding tightly to their six-year-old girl. They were all sobbing in grief.

"Let's pray," I said when they were seated, and as best I could, I talked to the Lord and asked him to comfort them. When I finished praying, the mother asked me to pray for their deceased little boy. Most believers are aware that the Word teaches that children go to be with God when they die.

"Are you Christians?" I asked.

"No," the mother replied, "I've been coming here for a couple weeks, but my husband doesn't believe in God. We came here because we didn't know where else to turn."

"You should know one thing," I told them. "If you don't ask Jesus into your hearts . . . you'll probably become bitter toward God because of what has happened. But if you ask Christ into your heart right now, he'll give you the peace that passes all human understanding. He'll get you through this trying time. Otherwise, you'll have such an emptiness that you won't know how to handle it."

Both parents and their small daughter were now crying uncontrollably. "Would you like to ask Jesus into your lives?" I asked.

"Yes, we would," they said.

They were all holding hands and crying as I led them in the sinner's prayer. It was a heavy experience—I was shaking as we prayed.

When they had left, I felt as if I had not done enough for them. But I knew I had to leave it in the Lord's hands. Two-and-a-half months later the mother came in to see me.

"Bruce," she began, "I came to talk to you, because I was sure you felt down after counseling us. But when you said, 'all things work together for good,' you weren't lying.

"My husband and I wanted you to know that although it was the most tragic thing that has ever happened to either of us, it was the only thing that could have caused us to ask Jesus into our lives. I would have kept coming as a Sunday Christian—as I had all my life. And as an athiest, my husband would not have responded in any other way.

"You can't believe the change in his life. He used to mock Christ at work. Now, he walks around with a smile on his face and shares his faith. Everyone knows he lost his son and no one can believe how he's taking it. He's a better worker, has a better personality, and is always happy.

"It hurts to think of our son and there will always be an empty place in our hearts for him, but we see how God has blessed our lives because of his death. It has healed us and brought our marriage back together. Bruce, we just wanted you to know what God has done."

College was teaching me about the ministry from a theological point of view. My work at Calvary was teaching me about the practical end. I especially enjoyed teaching the Bible studies and getting a chance to make the Word practical to people.

For months Debby and I had prayed that it would be God's will for me to officially come on staff at Calvary as a full-time minister receiving a full-time salary. Pastor Chuck began to look into my ministry and by the time summer was over, I was officially called as one of the pastors of the church. A little later the church ordained me. It had been a long wait—but it had been worth it.

As part of my increased responsibilities as a full-time pastor, I became involved in counseling with those who come forward at the Sunday morning services. One Sunday a young woman came forward sobbing. She asked me to pray for her boyfriend. He was a heroin addict and was in the state hospital. As we were talking it became obvious that she was not born again.

I asked her if she had a personal relationship with the Lord Jesus. She didn't.

"Would you like to invite Jesus to come into your life right now? That's the best first step you can make in helping your boyfriend with his drug problem."

She indicated her need for Christ and I led her through a basic sinner's prayer and into a new relationship with Jesus.

"Cheryl, the best thing I can suggest to you is the Bible study-discussion group meeting I lead every Sunday night at six o'clock. It's designed for anyone who has had a drug problem, or who has a loved one who is on drugs. You can discuss your problems with other Christians. We pray for one another."

That night, Cheryl came to our meeting. When she walked in, I realized that she was a face from my past. During the Bible study I tugged on my memory trying to figure out where I knew her from.

After the discussion and prayer time was over, Cheryl came up and gave me the name of her boyfriend and the address of the hospital he was in. "I would appreciate it if you would pray about visiting him. He's paranoid because he's ripped off so many people for thousands of dollars."

When she said those words, something clicked in my head, and instantly I knew this was the girl who had stolen $700 from me.

"Did you ever rip anybody off over at Bob's Restaurant in Costa Mesa?" I asked with a big knowing smile.

She jumped back. Her face turned white and her eyes dilated. Looking at me carefully, she asked, in a low voice. "Are you the guy we ripped off?! We were going to go out after we made the deal?"

"That's me!"

We both started laughing. After all this time we had run into each other.

"You don't hate me anymore?" she asked with a worried expression on her face.

"No, of course not. I'm a Christian now."

"I can't believe this!" she exclaimed. "I came to Calvary because I figured it was the one place I could come and not run into anyone from my past. And you were the one who led me to the Lord this morning!"

"Wow, that's the Lord!" I rejoiced. "Of all people to lead you to him!"

"I've had bad dreams for the past three years. I'm constantly dreaming about the terrible things that might have happened to all those people we stole from. We ripped off people for $50,000 at a time!"

Cheryl told me how she had been living a life of fear and how she had escaped being murdered when caught by some of the people she had bilked. She was certain many had contracts out for her death.

She looked me right in the eyes and asked seriously, "Do you want me to pay you back?"

"Oh, no," I laughed. "Forget it. It's on the Lord. I gave things like that up to the Lord a long time ago. He forgave me, so I forgive you."

Cheryl started sobbing. She was so overwhelmed by God's love. "My boyfriend would never believe this. Don't tell him you're one of the guys we ripped off. He doesn't believe anybody can forgive like that. He doesn't know that kind of love exists."

Cheryl had lived a life of wealth; she had driven the best cars. Now she had a simple eight-to-five job. She didn't even own a car—she walked to work.

"You know," she said, "I'm happier now than I've ever been before in my life. And now I have Jesus!"

As my ministry progressed, I possessed great joy, as any spiritual father would, watching the growth of those God had allowed me to lead to him. I had lost contact with many of the converts, but several continued to attend Calvary and I was able to watch their growth almost daily.

Mike Byrd was one of those who continued to grow dramatically. He had faced many trials and had weathered them all. He was now beginning to teach several Bible studies of his own and preparing to go to Bible college. It was exciting to see how turned on he had become. Truly God had blessed me with joy.

When people hear my story, they cannot comprehend how I can be a normal person today. After taking over 700 LSD trips and smoking marijuana almost every day for seven years, my brain should be gone today. But God in his grace has seen fit to restore my mind. After I became a Christian I spent many hours in the Bible, and the time spent meditating on God's Word restored my mind's ability to think and reason.

I trust that no one reading this book will envy the freedom I possessed while in the drug culture. Drugs and sensual living sucked me into a subtle trap. I had freedom, but it was a false freedom. I was actually under bondage to my way of life.

I was defensive and lied constantly. The good times never lasted. They were a counterfeit of genuine happiness. I never really knew love or real giving of myself. Everything I did, without exception, was motivated by my own selfish desires.

Some might argue I came to Christ only because I got busted. I praise God that I got busted so I would stop and think. But Christ was not merely an escape from prison. If I had to choose between my old life without Christ and prison with the Lord—I would definitely take prison and Christ. He provides the only true happiness.

I have lived two separate lives. The transformation God brought was so thorough that I am literally a different person now. I did many things in my drug dealing days that I am ashamed of today. Many, many of my exploits have purposely been left out of this book. Like the Apostle Paul I grieve over my past life and the lives I helped ruin.

I sometimes marvel that the Lord chose to save me, but like the Apostle Paul, I have been forgiven. And it is very true that he who is forgiven much loves much. My prayer today is that my life and ministry may reach more people for Christ than my pleasure selling days reached for Satan. If you have become a Christian through reading this book, I'd love to hear from you. Write me in care of the publishers. May God be praised!